HADRIAN'S WALL AND K

INCLUDING
Bellingham, Bolam, Chesters, Corstopi[...]
Housesteads, Kershope, Kielder Castle, [...] ..., ..o..... iyne
Valley, Once Brewed, Vindolanda, Wall (v....ye,, wallington Hall and Wark.

This guide book contains exact, easy to follow directions for the motorist to explore some of Britain's least known countryside which has for almost two thousand years echoed to the battle cries of Roman Invaders, Viking Marauders and Border Reivers. Northumbria, the core of an ancient Saxon Kingdom is an area of contrast dominated by Hadrian's Wall (see notes on page 12), the northernmost limit of the mighty Roman Empire, and the Border Forest, the largest man-made forest in Europe. Housesteads, Vindolanda, Chesters, Corstopitum are exciting Roman excavations, contrasting with the ruined castles and abbeys of Thirlwall, Lanercost, Hermitage, Bewcastle and the sumptuous elegance of Wallington Hall; all in an area of breathtaking beauty. Stone-built villages and friendly market towns provide yet further contrast.

The Circular Route shown on the Key Map opposite covers 150 miles. Alternatively the day visitor will find main arteries leading to the key points on the tour fast and traffic free. The entire route contains so many places of interest that it would take the average motorist several days to complete, if all were to be visited.

However, the tourist can be selective, and it is also possible to break the tour into two circuits of 120 miles Hexham-Hadrians Wall-Bewcastle-Kielder and back to Hexham; and Hexham-Bellingham-Wanneys-Wallington-Hexham, a 65 mile circuit. Overnight stops can be made in varied accommodation from farmhouse, bed and breakfast, to country hotel. Accommodation is not as sparse as it used to be, as the area has become far better known to the tourist. Hexham Tourist Information Centre can assist you to find accommodation [☎ (0434) 605225].

HOW TO USE YOUR BOOK ON THE ROUTE

Each double page makes up a complete picture of the country ahead of you. On the left you will find a one inch to the mile strip map, with the route marked by a series of dashes. Direction is always from top to bottom, so that the map may be looked at in conjunction with the 'directions to the driver', with which it is cross referenced by a letter itemising each junction point. This enables the driver to have exact guidance every time an opportunity for changing direction occurs.

With mileage intervals shown, the driver should even have warning when to expect these 'moments of decision', and if a signpost exists we have used this to help you, with the 'Signposted' column. However re-signing is always in progress, and this may lead to slight differences in sign marking in some cases.... So beware of freshly erected signs.

We have also included a description of the towns and villages through which you will pass, together with some photographs to illustrate the route.

To gain full enjoyment from these journeys be prepared to leave your car as often as possible. The Northumberland National Park and the Border Forest are very accessible and footpaths and bridleways abound. The air is exhilarating and even the most inexperienced walker is able to enjoy the thrill of a walk along a Roman road, over heather-clad moor or through woodlands with the hardware of history ever present.

Compiled by NOEL and HILDA TURNBULL
Third Edition Revisions. Hexham Tourist Information Centre
Series Editor PETER TITCHMARSH

Map 1

Ref	kms/Miles	Directions	Sign-posted
A		Depart from Hexham Market Place — Abbey, by left of Moot Hall A6079 via Hallstile Bank (one-way street)	Chollerford
	.2	Take 3rd exit at roundabout at foot of hill	Carlise
	.2	Forward at mini-roundabout to…	A69/A6079
		Cross railway bridge and then River Tyne Bridge, and…	Carlisle/Newcastle
		Continue to A69 trunk road interchange	
B	.5	Turn left with care on to A69	Carlisle
C	.7	Turn right on to A6079	Bellingham Otterburn Hadrian's Wa
	.4	Pass Acomb Village	
	2.2	Continue to Wall Village	
	.1	Turn sharp right off A6079 to Wall Village Green	No sign
	.1	Leave by left turn off Village Green and rejoin A6079	No sign
	.5	Continue north on A6079	No sign
		Layby on right and footpath to Brunton Roman Turret (100 yards)	
D	.2	Turn left at X-roads on to B6318	Chollerford
	.2	Immediately before crossing River North Tyne Bridge, footpath on left to Chesters Roman Bridge Abutment (500 yards)	
		Cross Bridge, George Hotel on right	
E	.1	At roundabout take first exit left on to B6318	Greenhead Roman Wall
		(BUT TAKE SECOND LEFT, ON TO B6320 IF YOU WISH TO TAKE DIRECT ROUTE TO BELLINGHAM, LINKING ON TO MAP 10, POINT D (12 MILES). THIS PROVIDES AN EAST CIRCLE ROUTE BACK TO HEXHAM, USING MAPS 11, 12, 13, 14 AND 15)	
F	.4	Turn left into Chesters Roman Fort	Chesters
	1.5	After visiting Chesters, turn right, re-joining B6318	National Park
	1.2	The B6318 runs on top of the course of Hadrian's Wall	
		Total mileage on this map: 8.5	

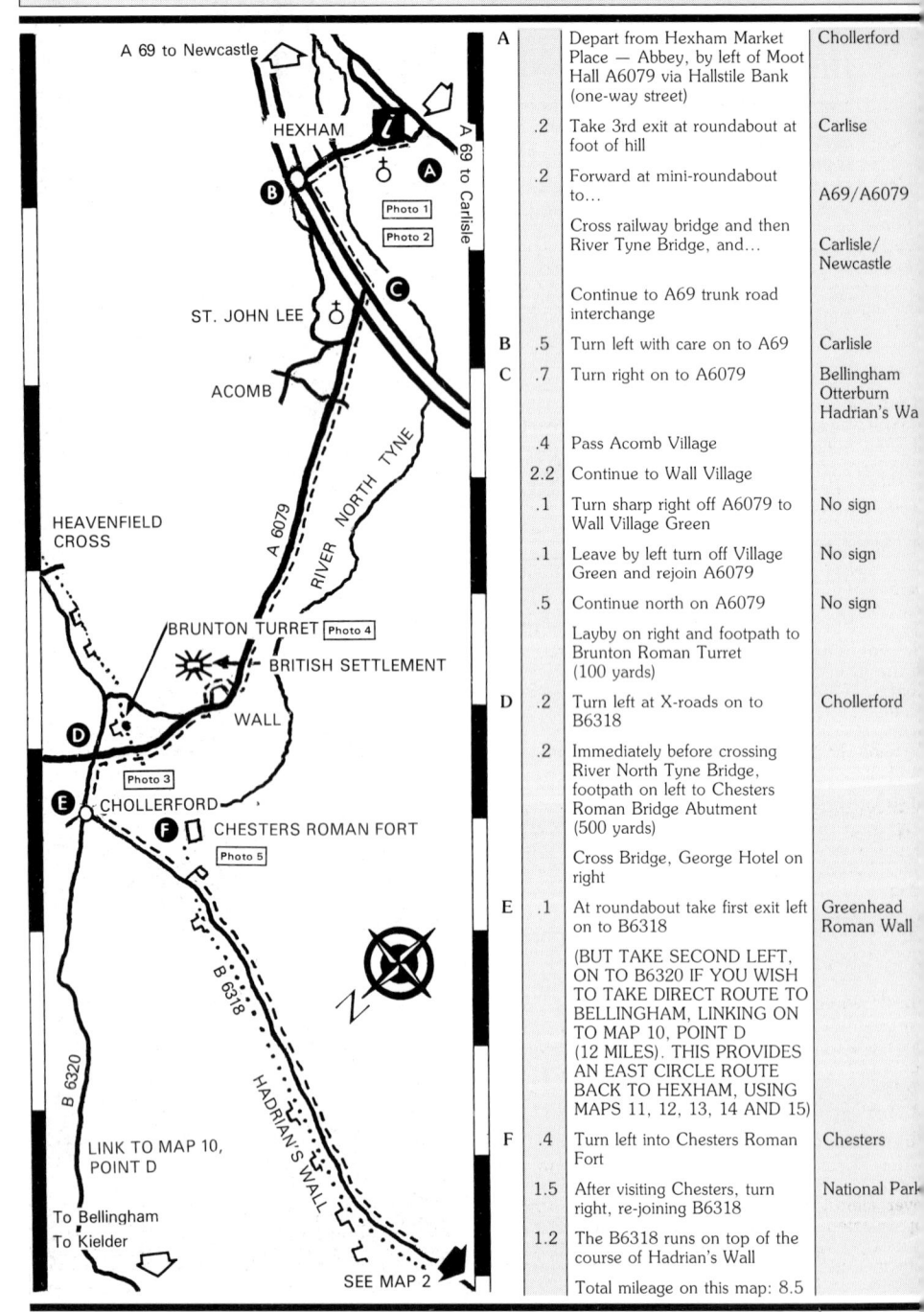

CROWN COPYRIGHT RESERVED

On Route

Map 1

From the ancient market town of Hexham, a gateway to Roman Wall country and the Northumberland National Park, this route passes through fertile undulating countryside where the scent of Roman history fills the air and every grey stone building has its own story to tell. North of Hexham, Hadrian's Wall snakes its way westwards crossing the River Tyne at Chollerford. Stretches of original wall, nearly two thousand years old, remains of turrets and milecastles and extensive excavations at Chesters Fort provide an absorbing insight into the Roman way of life during the occupation of Britain. At Hexham Abbey are reminders of the part Northumbria played in nurturing the spread of Christianity in the 7th and 8th centuries.

Hexham

St. Wilfred founded a church here in AD 680 built of stones taken from Hadrian's Wall. The humble church soon grew in importance to become an abbey which remains today in all its architectural splendour. Features in the Abbey include a Saxon crypt and the "Frith Stool" on which Saxon Kings were crowned. The Moot Hall dates from the early 14th century and was originally the gatehouse of the castle in which were housed the bailiffs of the Archbishops of York. It was used as a Court House until 1838. Nearby is the Manor Office, which was built as a prison in 1330. This now houses a Tourist Information Centre (open all the year) and also the interesting Middle March Centre, which tells the turbulent story of the Anglo-Scottish Border Country, through much of which we shall be travelling.

There are pleasant walks by the River Tyne, golf and fishing.

Wall Village

A most attractive grouping of stone cottages around a series of greens. The earthworks of a Native British Settlement are set on the crag high above the village.

Brunton Turret

Roman remains seven feet high, including turret 26b and a stretch of wall.

Chollerford

Immediately before crossing the North Tyne River an easy walk leads to the remarkable remains of the Roman bridge abutment where the line of the Wall crossed the Tyne. This was first excavated in 1860 and is well-known for its Roman phallic carving.

Chesters

The Roman remains of the Station known as Cilurnum and the largest fort in Northumberland, over almost six acres. Extensive remains include sophisticated bathhouse, headquarters building, barracks, granaries and other buildings. The museum contains one of the country's most important collection of Roman exhibits.

1. In the Tourist Information Centre at Hexham

2. Hexham—Entrance to the T.I.C. and the Middle March Centre

3. Roman Bridge Abutment, Chollerford

4. Brunton Turret   An English Heritage Photograph

5. Chesters Roman Fort   An English Heritage Photograph

3

Map 2

Ref	kms/Miles	Directions	Sign-posted
		Continue west on B6318	
A	.9	Turn left into car park for Brocolitia Mithraeum Temple at Carrawburgh. Follow easy footpath (300 yards)	Brocolitia
		Now re-join B6318	
	.7	Note straightness of Roman Road and views in all directions	
B	1.0	Site of Milecastle 33 on right	
	.1	Lough (Lake) at Shield on the Wall on left	
C	.6	Road bears left leaving course of wall still clearly visible to north	
		Site of Milecastle 34 on right	
D	.4	Continue past Sewingshields. Site of Milecastle 35 and Turret 34(b) well over to right	
E	1.8	Turn right into car park for Housestead Roman Fort. Toilets. Surfaced footpath across fields leads to Fort, Museum and Wall, 900 yards each way. Interpretive Centre at Car Park	Housesteads
		Now re-join B6318	
F	.9	Straight, not left, keeping on B6318 (But turn left if you wish to visit Bardon Mill and Allen Banks. For route details see opposite page)	Greenhead
	2.0	Arrive at Once Brewed National Park Information Centre crossroads (See Map 3)	
		At Once Brewed crossroads turn left off B6318, then second right into the National Park Information Centre Car Park	Vindolanda
		Note Hadrian's Wall clearly on skyline ridge to the north, following the fiercely undulating ground. Milecastle 39 nestles to the left of some particularly spectacular undulations	
		Total mileage on this map: 8.5	

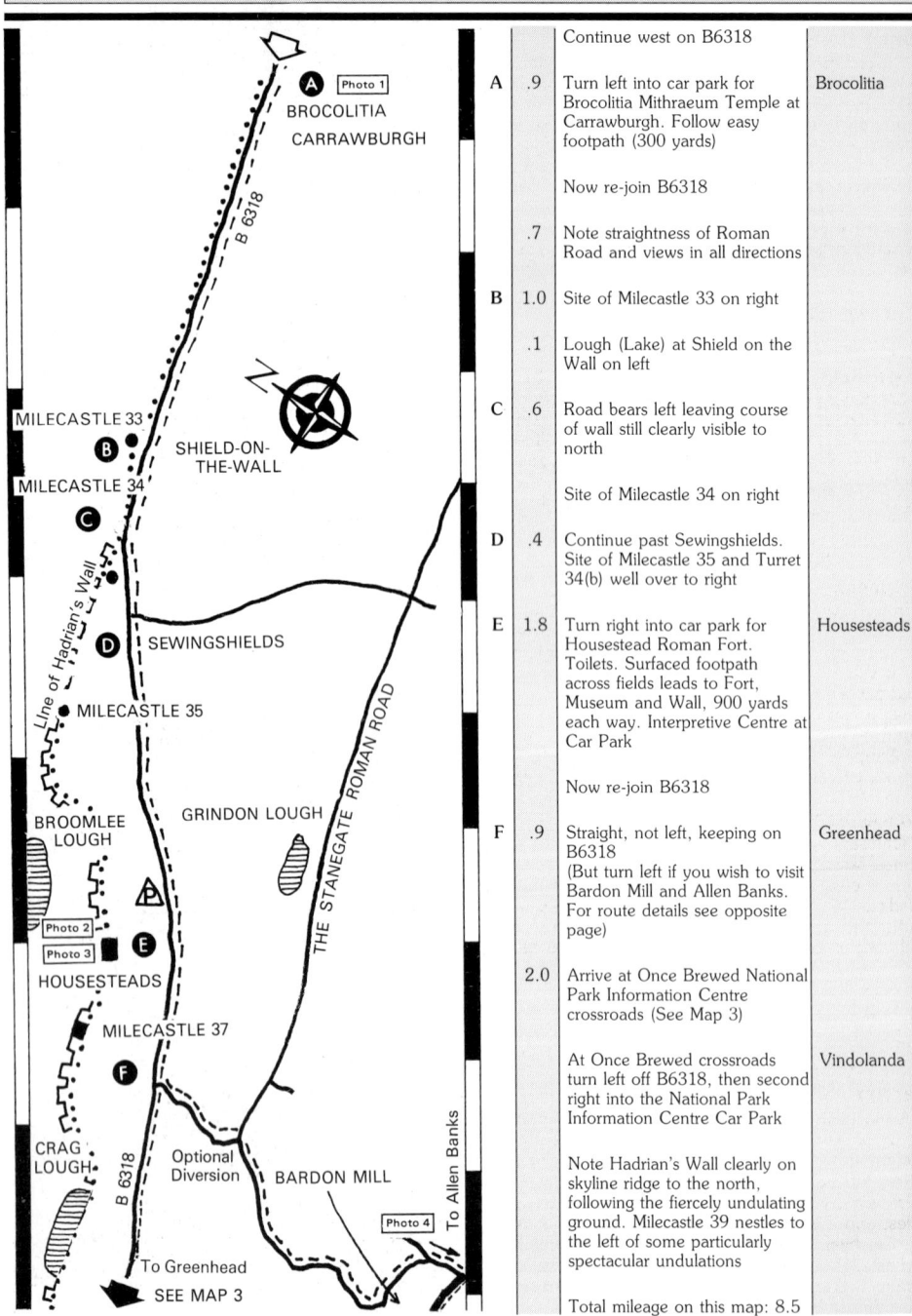

CROWN COPYRIGHT RESERVED

On Route

Map 2

The fertile valley of the River Tyne gives way to dramatic, stark moorland, where the barren, almost treeless landscape is scarred by rocky outcrops and dominated by the course of Hadrian's Wall snaking over the Whin Sill, a natural barrier which crosses from east to west.

The excavated Temple of Mithras can be seen at Carrawburgh; and Housesteads, the best known excavated fort is reached by an exhilarating walk across green fields. Then the route descends to the fertile valley of the South Tyne and a detour to the tranquillity of Allen Banks.

Carrawburgh

Originally called Brocolitia meaning "Brockholes" the site was formerly frequented by badgers. A huge grassy mound denotes the outline of the fort but the dry summer of 1949 revealed to the south west of the fort one of the most outstanding of Roman discoveries — a temple to the sun god Mithras. Founded circa AD 205 the temple is completely excavated although the altars and sculptures are replicas. To the west of the wall surrounding the field is an equally remarkable find. Here in 1876 Coventina's Well yielded more than 14,000 Roman coins and many other treasures.

Sewingshields

In just over two miles from Carrawburgh the road bears left and the route of Hadrian's Wall is clearly visible shooting off at a tangent towards the high crags of the Whin Sill to the north. Half a mile further on the road passes through an area steeped in legend where Sewingshields Castle once stood. Romantics believe that King Arthur, Guinevere and the lords and ladies of Arthur's Court are imprisoned in some underground cell awaiting their release which can only be summoned by the blowing of a mystic bugle.

Housesteads

The best preserved of the Roman forts, originally named Vercovicium. The site of the fort covers five acres and many buildings are clearly visible including headquarters buildings, granaries, barracks and, particularly intriguing, the latrines, which reveal a high degree of sophistication. Hadrian's Wall passes to the north of the Fort and energetic walkers can traverse the top of the wall for several miles westwards. There is a large car park and an excellent shop and information centre. Walk along the Wall a short way westwards to obtain the classic view from Cuddy's Crag (see picture on page 7).

Bardon Mill (Optional diversion)

A pleasant village beside the South Tyne River on the main A69 road. Its name is derived from an ancient woollen mill. There is now a pottery here.

Allen Banks (Optional diversion)

Drive eastwards on the A69 from Bardon Mill for .8 miles, and then turn right (sign — Ridley Hall). After 5 miles bear left at Ridley Hall (sign — Plankey Mill) and after .2 miles enter Allen Banks National Trust Picnic Area by the beautifully wooded banks of the River Allen.

1. Mithraic Temple, Brocolitia

2. Housesteads Fort — An aerial View
An English Heritage Photograph

3. Granary, Housesteads Fort

4. Allen Banks

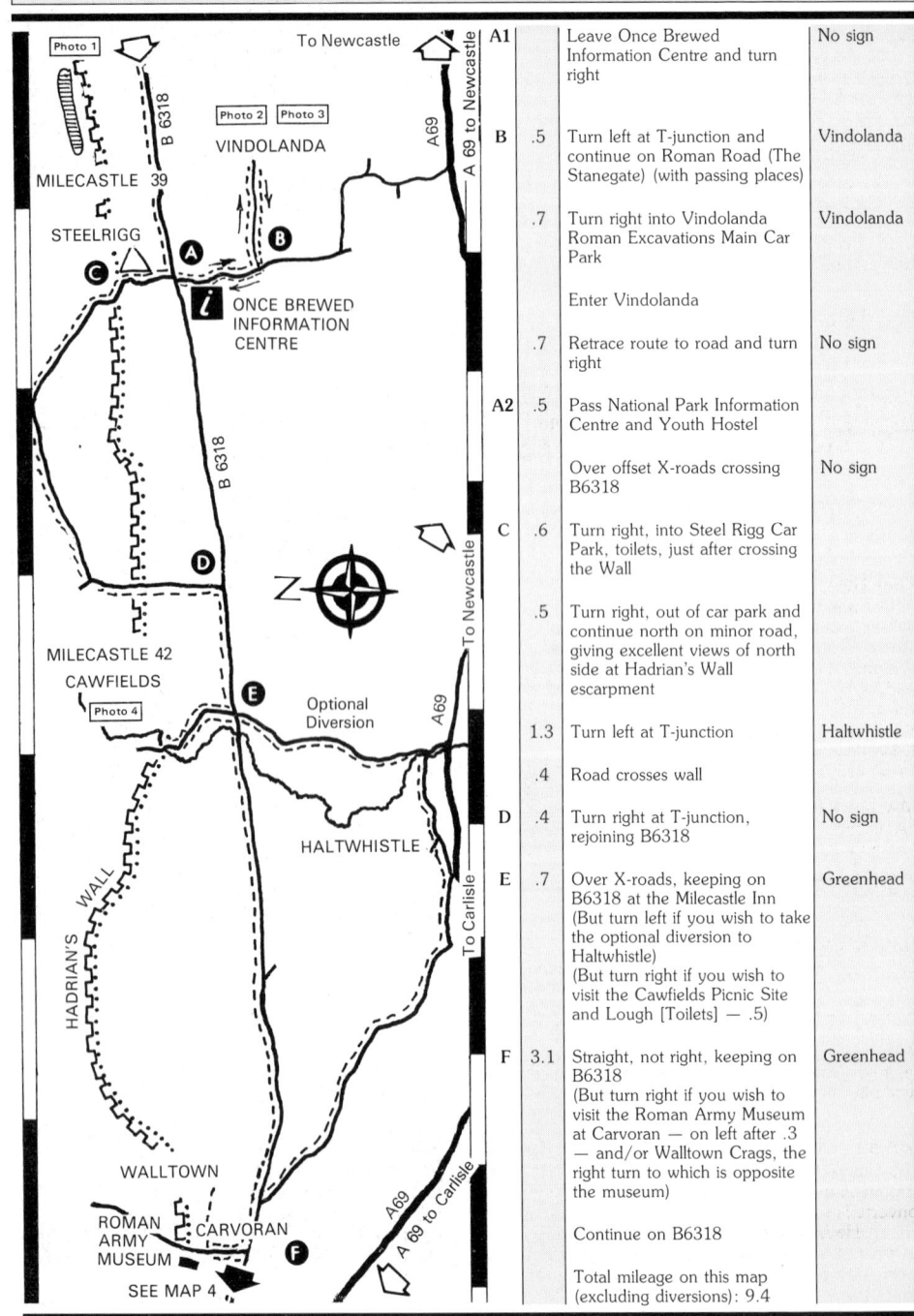

Map 3

Ref	kms/Miles	Directions	Sign-posted
A1		Leave Once Brewed Information Centre and turn right	No sign
B	.5	Turn left at T-junction and continue on Roman Road (The Stanegate) (with passing places)	Vindolanda
	.7	Turn right into Vindolanda Roman Excavations Main Car Park	Vindolanda
		Enter Vindolanda	
	.7	Retrace route to road and turn right	No sign
A2	.5	Pass National Park Information Centre and Youth Hostel	
		Over offset X-roads crossing B6318	No sign
C	.6	Turn right, into Steel Rigg Car Park, toilets, just after crossing the Wall	
	.5	Turn right, out of car park and continue north on minor road, giving excellent views of north side at Hadrian's Wall escarpment	
	1.3	Turn left at T-junction	Haltwhistle
	.4	Road crosses wall	
D	.4	Turn right at T-junction, rejoining B6318	No sign
E	.7	Over X-roads, keeping on B6318 at the Milecastle Inn (But turn left if you wish to take the optional diversion to Haltwhistle) (But turn right if you wish to visit the Cawfields Picnic Site and Lough [Toilets] — .5)	Greenhead
F	3.1	Straight, not right, keeping on B6318 (But turn right if you wish to visit the Roman Army Museum at Carvoran — on left after .3 — and/or Walltown Crags, the right turn to which is opposite the museum)	Greenhead
		Continue on B6318	
		Total mileage on this map (excluding diversions): 9.4	

CROWN COPYRIGHT RESERVED

On Route

Map 3

This route takes us through the heart of Wall country where unique reminders of Northumbria's Roman occupation are seen at Vindolanda — the fort and town situated on the Roman Stanegate Road a mile south of Hadrian's Wall. It returns to the Wall at Steel Rigg and then on to Cawfields and Walltown Crags leading to some of the most spectacular scenery in all Britain.

After descending to the peaceful market town of Haltwhistle the route continues west following the line of Hadrian's Wall.

Vindolanda

Although south of the wall, the excavations of this 3rd and 4th century fort and town give a remarkable picture of Roman life. In addition to the extensive excavations, a full scale replica of sections of Hadrian's Wall have been constructed in turf and stone and the museum houses unique finds from the site including wooden writing tablets and the largest collection of Roman leather in Europe which has survived here as a result of special soil conditions. Excavations, most summer months.

Steel Rigg

The breathtaking view from Steel Rigg as the Wall snakes precariously eastwards along Peel Crags to the sombre blue waters of Crag Lough is one of the highlights of any visit to 'Wall Country'. If they have a head for heights, energetic visitors can walk along the Wall as far as Housesteads passing the site of Turret 39A to the remains of Turret 36B. Remains of Milecastles 39 and 37 are also clearly visible.

Cawfields (Optional Diversion)

A diversion for half a mile leads to Cawfields Picnic Area by a delightful lake in the shadows of the Great Whin Sill which takes the Wall eastwards to the well-preserved Milecastle 42.

Haltwhistle (Optional Diversion)

A pleasant town situated where the Haltwhistle Burn joins the South Tyne and a good centre for touring Hadrian's Wall. The church dates from the 13th century and is, unusually, without a tower. The town's name is derived from Hantwysel meaning "the watch on the high mound". There is an open-air swimming pool here.

Roman Army Museum and Walltown Crags

The Fort of Carvoran is not displayed, but the farmbuildings of the adjacent farm have been converted into a Museum of the Roman Army, and its role on Hadrian's Wall. Well worth a visit.

One of the finest stretches of wall together with a Turret (45A), which experts believe was constructed before the Wall, probably as a signalling outpost.

1. Hadrian's Wall — The view from Cuddy's Crag towards Housesteads (see page 5)
An English Heritage Photograph

2. Hadrian's Wall Replica Vindolanda

3. Leatherwear at Vindolanda Museum

4. Milecastle 42 at Cawfields
An English Heritage Photograph

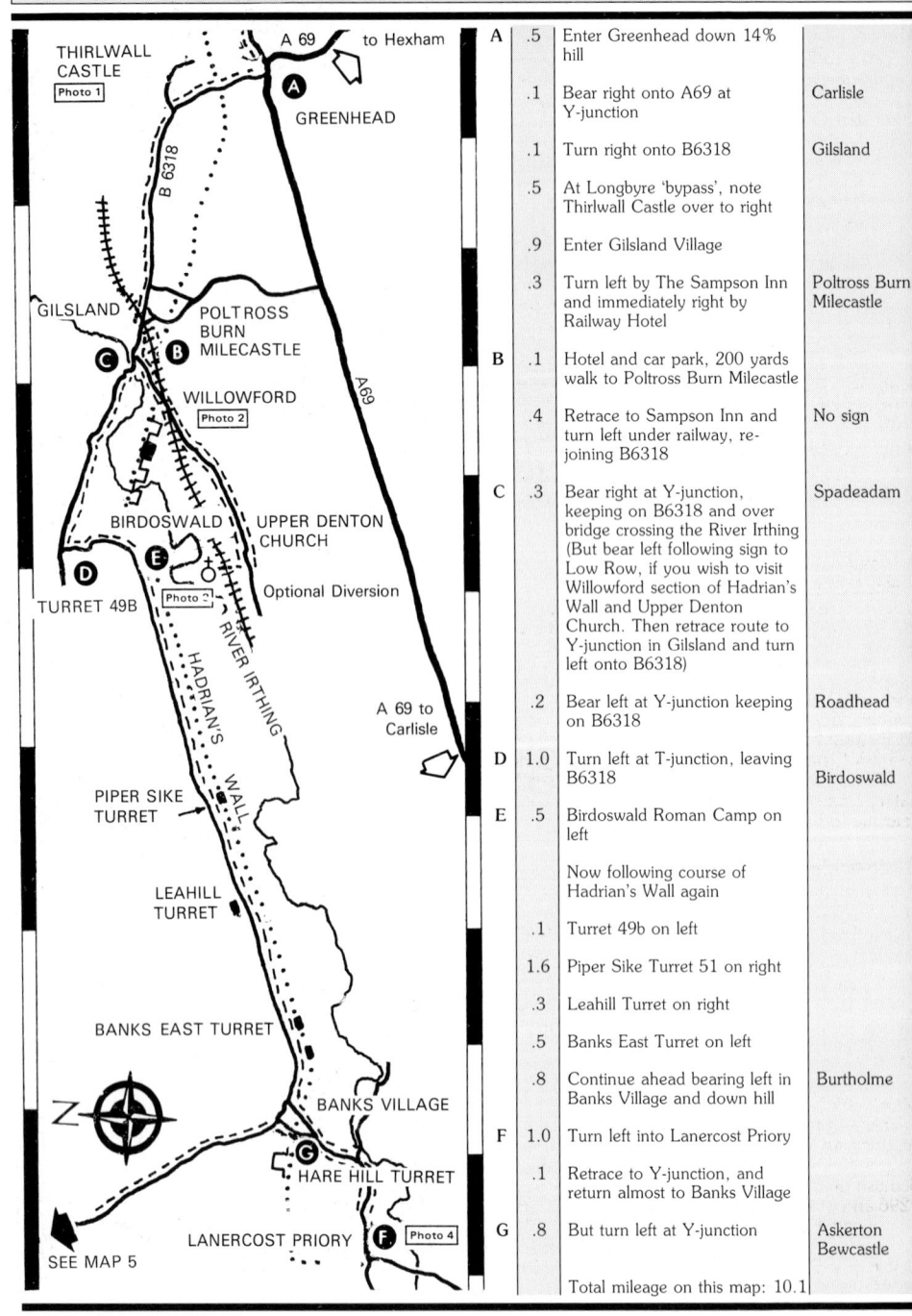

Map 4

	kms Ref Miles	Directions	Sign-posted
A	.5	Enter Greenhead down 14% hill	
	.1	Bear right onto A69 at Y-junction	Carlisle
	.1	Turn right onto B6318	Gilsland
	.5	At Longbyre 'bypass', note Thirlwall Castle over to right	
	.9	Enter Gilsland Village	
	.3	Turn left by The Sampson Inn and immediately right by Railway Hotel	Poltross Burn Milecastle
B	.1	Hotel and car park, 200 yards walk to Poltross Burn Milecastle	
	.4	Retrace to Sampson Inn and turn left under railway, re-joining B6318	No sign
C	.3	Bear right at Y-junction, keeping on B6318 and over bridge crossing the River Irthing (But bear left following sign to Low Row, if you wish to visit Willowford section of Hadrian's Wall and Upper Denton Church. Then retrace route to Y-junction in Gilsland and turn left onto B6318)	Spadeadam
	.2	Bear left at Y-junction keeping on B6318	Roadhead
D	1.0	Turn left at T-junction, leaving B6318	Birdoswald
E	.5	Birdoswald Roman Camp on left	
		Now following course of Hadrian's Wall again	
	.1	Turret 49b on left	
	1.6	Piper Sike Turret 51 on right	
	.3	Leahill Turret on right	
	.5	Banks East Turret on left	
	.8	Continue ahead bearing left in Banks Village and down hill	Burtholme
F	1.0	Turn left into Lanercost Priory	
	.1	Retrace to Y-junction, and return almost to Banks Village	
G	.8	But turn left at Y-junction	Askerton Bewcastle
		Total mileage on this map: 10.1	

CROWN COPYRIGHT RESERVED

On Route

Map 4

After our route crosses the county boundary between Northumberland and Cumbria, we visit Thirlwall Castle, and impressive stretches of wall wend over more gentle countryside, lush and fertile in contrast to the barren moors to the east. Battle and bloodshed by Romans and Border Reivers are forgotten in the tranquillity of the ancient church at Upper Denton and the silent cloisters of Lanercost Priory.

1. Thirlwall Castle

Thirlwall Castle (Not open to public)

Built of Roman stone its name is derived from the action of the Scots "thirling" (throwing down) Hadrian's Wall. Edward I visited Thirlwall in 1306. It played its part in the Border forays before falling into disrepair in the 17th century, and is said to be haunted.

Poltross Burn Milecastle at Gilsland

Milecastle 48 was constructed during the early part of the reign of Hadrian and was occupied until the end of the 4th century.

Willowford (Optional diversion)

Fine stretches of wall with easy access, together with the remains of Turrets 48A and 48B. Remains of the Roman bridge abutment are visible by the River Irthing.

2. Turret at Willowford

Upper Denton Church (Optional diversion)

Constructed of stones from Hadrian's Wall and Birdoswald Fort the church holds only 50 people and is one of the smallest parish churches in England. Peculiarly there is no vestry and the chancel arch dating from Saxon times is a reconstruction of the gateway to the Roman Fort at Birdoswald.

Birdoswald Fort

This fort was intended to guard the Irthing Bridge and its Roman name was Camboglanna meaning Crook Bank. The wall of the north-west tower is fourteen courses high and the main east gate is regarded as the best preserved of all. The site is believed by romantics to be Camlan, where King Arthur fought his last battle. The Birdoswald, Piper Sike, Leahill and Banks East turrets all skirt the road westwards from the Fort.

3. Upper Denton Church

Lanercost Priory

This was founded in 1166 by Robert de Vaux for Augustinian Canons who led a predominantly peaceful existence in spite of plundering raids by Scottish marauders. The cloisters were burned in 1296 and a year later William Wallace laid it waste, an act repeated by King David II of Scotland in 1346. Edward I made several visits en route to Newcastle or Carlisle, being taken ill while at the Priory in 1306 and staying for six months.

4. Lanercost Priory

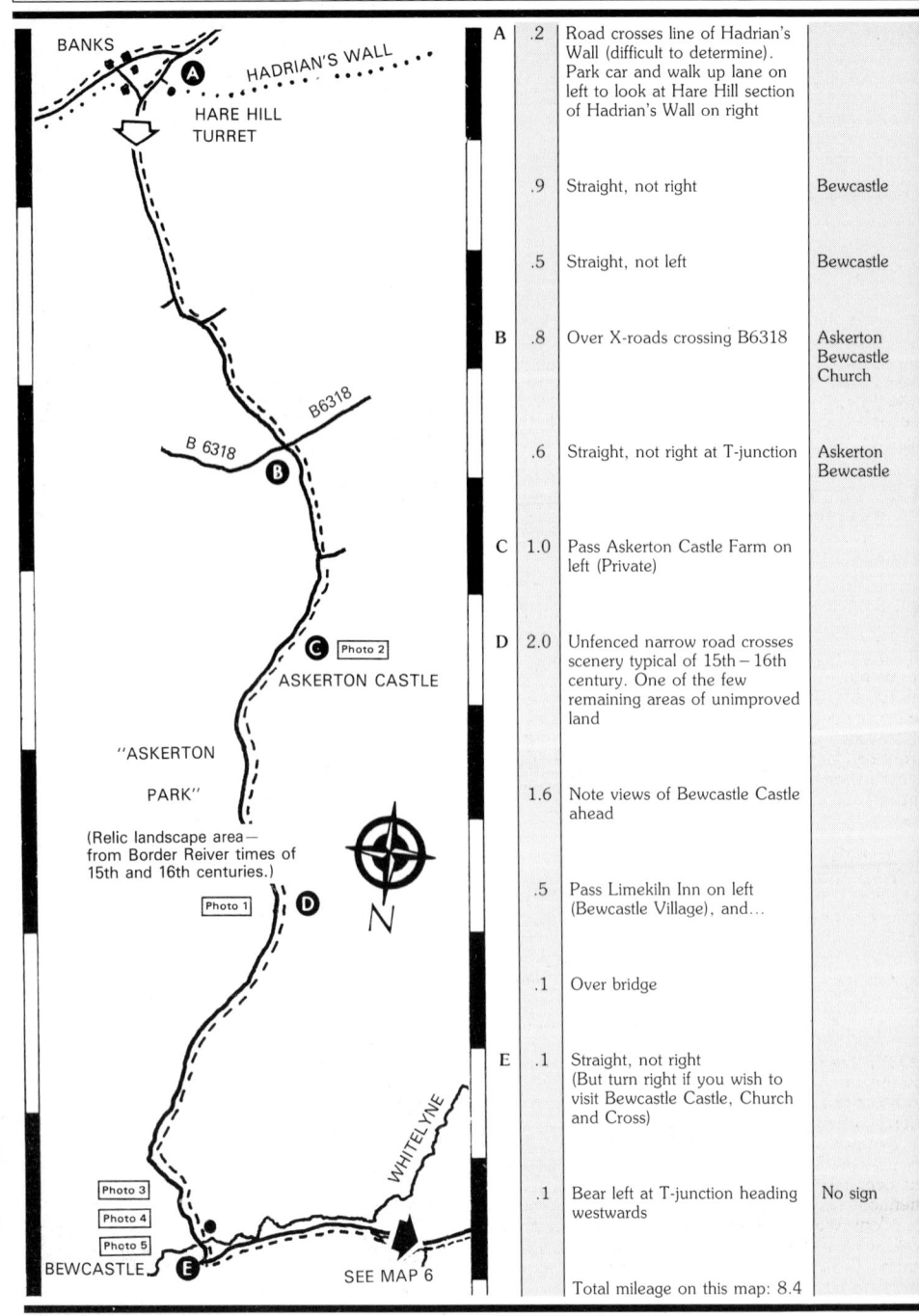

Map 5

	kms Ref Miles	Directions	Sign-posted
A	.2	Road crosses line of Hadrian's Wall (difficult to determine). Park car and walk up lane on left to look at Hare Hill section of Hadrian's Wall on right	
	.9	Straight, not right	Bewcastle
	.5	Straight, not left	Bewcastle
B	.8	Over X-roads crossing B6318	Askerton Bewcastle Church
	.6	Straight, not right at T-junction	Askerton Bewcastle
C	1.0	Pass Askerton Castle Farm on left (Private)	
D	2.0	Unfenced narrow road crosses scenery typical of 15th – 16th century. One of the few remaining areas of unimproved land	
	1.6	Note views of Bewcastle Castle ahead	
	.5	Pass Limekiln Inn on left (Bewcastle Village), and...	
	.1	Over bridge	
E	.1	Straight, not right (But turn right if you wish to visit Bewcastle Castle, Church and Cross)	
	.1	Bear left at T-junction heading westwards	No sign
		Total mileage on this map: 8.4	

Map labels: BANKS, HADRIAN'S WALL, HARE HILL TURRET, B6318, ASKERTON CASTLE, "ASKERTON PARK" (Relic landscape area—from Border Reiver times of 15th and 16th centuries.), WHITELYNE, BEWCASTLE, SEE MAP 6

CROWN COPYRIGHT RESERVED

On Route

Map 5

A route of changing scenic splendour. From the Cumbrian plains, through meadowland and sleepy farms, past the ancient church at Bewcastle and the private castellated residence at Askerton before forsaking gentle Cumbria for the harsh fell country beyond. These isolated and bleak hills are a perfect setting for the awesome ruin of Bewcastle Castle and the famous Cross in the nearby churchyard.

Hare Hill Turret

Retracing our route from Lanercost Priory almost to the hamlet of Banks village, the line of Hadrian's Wall is crossed. At Hare Hill is the highest remaining section of Hadrian's Wall — 16 courses high. The bumps, mounds and hummocks in the vicinity indicate just how much more of Hadrian's Wall remains to be exposed and conserved from beneath the turf.

Askerton Castle (Not open to public)

A 16th century castellated mansion now a private farm. Note the unusual weather vane on the barn nearby.

A Historic Landscape — Askerton "Park"

This wild area of rough open grassland through which your narrow unfenced road takes you, could not be more inappropriately named as "Park". In fact this type of landscape is now most rare. Never having been enclosed, it still presents us today with the type of landscape the border reivers and raiders would have seen in the 15 and 16th centuries, when the wild Scots and English were plundering each other's cattle and sheep.

Bewcastle

The Bewcastle Cross situated in the church yard is believed to date from the late 7th century. The head of the cross has disappeared but the splendid carvings on the shaft are the main cause of historians' interest. On the southern side are runes which have puzzled experts for centuries. The north side has general decoration while the east side is decorated with grotesque animals and birds. Historians have turned their attention to the west face which features four panels, three of biblical influence and the fourth an inscription. The runes commemorate King Alcfrith who was the son of Oswi who died in AD 670. The church is typically 18th century.

The ruins of "Beuth's Castle" is not the first building on the site. The first castle was undoubtedly wooden but centuries before that, the Romans turned their attentions to this place which was linked by the "Maidens Way" to Birdoswald Camp on Hadrian's Wall. Roman stones went into the present structure, a true Border fortress built some 600 years ago to guard an important Reiver's way.

1. The ancient natural landscape of Border Reiver times

2. Askerton Castle

3. Bewcastle Castle

4 and 5. Two views of Bewcastle Cross

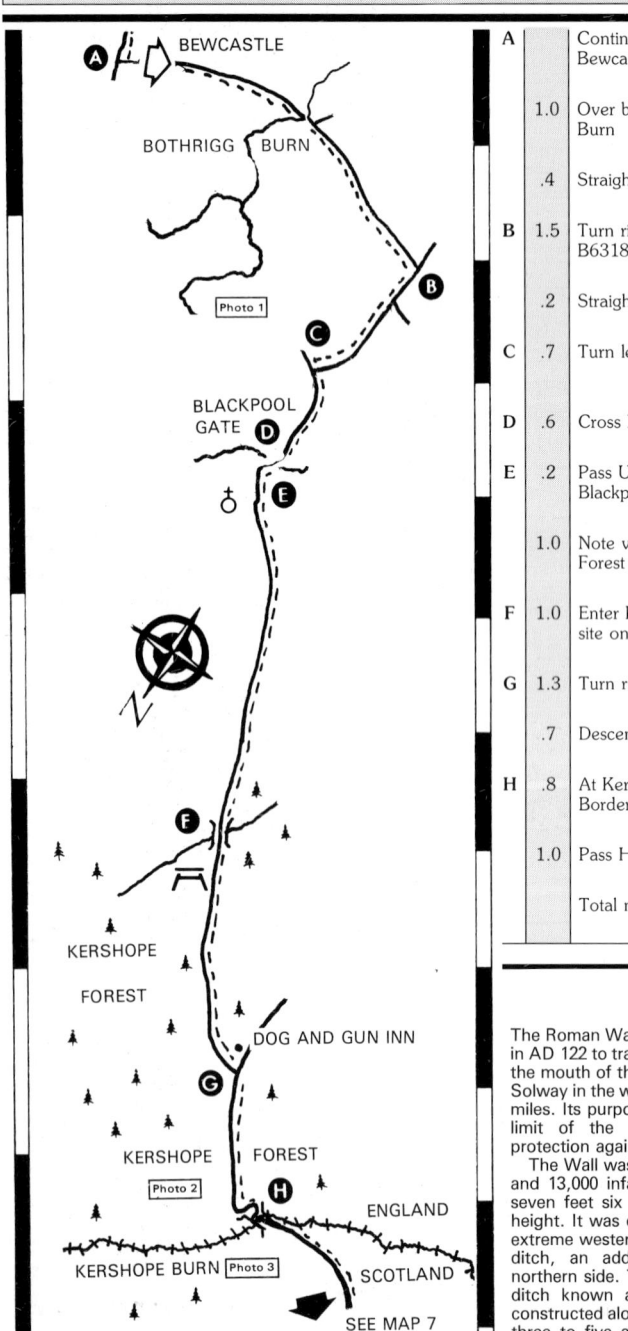

Map 6

Ref	kms/Miles	Directions	Sign-posted
A		Continue westwards from Bewcastle	
	1.0	Over bridge crossing Bothrigg Burn	
	.4	Straight, not left at Y-junction	Newcastleton
B	1.5	Turn right at T-junction on to B6318	Newcastleton
	.2	Straight, not left, leaving B6318	Newcastleton
C	.7	Turn left at Y-junction	Blackpool Gate
D	.6	Cross River Black Lyne	
E	.2	Pass United Reform Church in Blackpool Gate hamlet	
	1.0	Note views ahead of Kershope Forest	
F	1.0	Enter Kershope Forest (picnic site on right)	
G	1.3	Turn right at Dog and Gun Inn	Kershopefoot
	.7	Descend hill 1 in 6	
H	.8	At Kershope Bridge cross Border into Scotland	No sign
	1.0	Pass Hill End	

Total mileage on this map: 10.4

Hadrian's Wall —

The Roman Wall was built by order of Emperor Hadrian in AD 122 to traverse the narrow neck of land from near the mouth of the River Tyne in the east to Bowness on Solway in the west, a distance of 73 miles, or 80 Roman miles. Its purpose was to demarcate the northernmost limit of the mighty Roman Empire and provide protection against the wild inhabitants to the north.

The Wall was manned by a garrison of 5,500 cavalry and 13,000 infantry. Its general dimensions averaged seven feet six inches in thickness and fifteen feet in height. It was constructed of local stone although the extreme western sector was built of turf. A 'V' shaped ditch, an additional protection, skirted the wall's northern side. To its south was another flat bottomed ditch known as the Vallum. Seventeen forts were constructed along the Wall, each covering an area from three to five and a half acres. At each Roman mile

CROWN COPYRIGHT RESERVED

On Route

Map 6

This route traverses much wild and inhospitable country. Bleak moors and fells to the north of Bewcastle were the true "Debateable Lands" where law and order was based for centuries on "survival of the fittest". Uneasy peace now reigns in uncanny silence, but there is beauty in the desolation. A wild, untameable beauty where rolling fells are watered by the crystal waters of Bothrigg Burn, White Lyne Water and Black Lyne.

Tumbled stone buildings, now hardly recognisable, may once have been a Pele Tower and the evocative names of hill and vale are steeped in history and mystery — Blackpool Gate — Black Knors — Black Rigg, and a sense of foreboding awaits round every bend in the narrow twisting roads. From stark moorland the road ahead beckons the visitor into the eerie chasms of Kershope Forest.

Blackpool Gate

Nothing is known of the derivation of the name of this tiny hamlet except that it could be taken literally as being situated on Black Lyne Water.

Kershope Forest

This forms part of the expansive Border Forest and amenities include picnic areas, particularly at the point where the road first enters the woodland. The Kershope Burn determines the Anglo–Scottish Border for several miles. The mouth of the burn, a few miles west of our route where it joins Liddel Water, saw the famous meeting of the Wardens of the Marches in March 1596 and the resultant capture by the English of the notorious Kinmont Willie, a feared Scottish Reiver, only a day after a truce had been declared. The Middle March runs from the head of Kershope Burn in the Larriston Fells to Auchope Cairn on Cheviot. Learn more about the history of this turbulent area at the Middle March Centre in Hexham (see page 3).

— a General Note

1,620 yards) a milecastle was constructed as sentries' quarters and signalling posts. Between each milecastle were two, twenty foot square towers, known as turrets.

Although almost 90% of the Wall remains unexposed, those sections including forts, milecastle and turrets which are visible provide a vivid insight into the sophisticated life enjoyed during almost four hundred years of Roman occupation. The central sector is by far the most interesting and informative, but the route of the Wall can be walked its entire length. The Wall forms the Southern boundary to the Northumberland National Park which stretches northwards over four hundred square miles to the Cheviot Hills and the Scottish Border, remote and contrasting hill country which for thousands of years has been a natural border.

For further information, Guide Books and where to stay details, contact Hexham Tourist Information Centre ☎ (0434) 605255

1. White Lyne Water

2. Kershope Forest

3. Kershope Bridge on the Anglo–Scottish Border

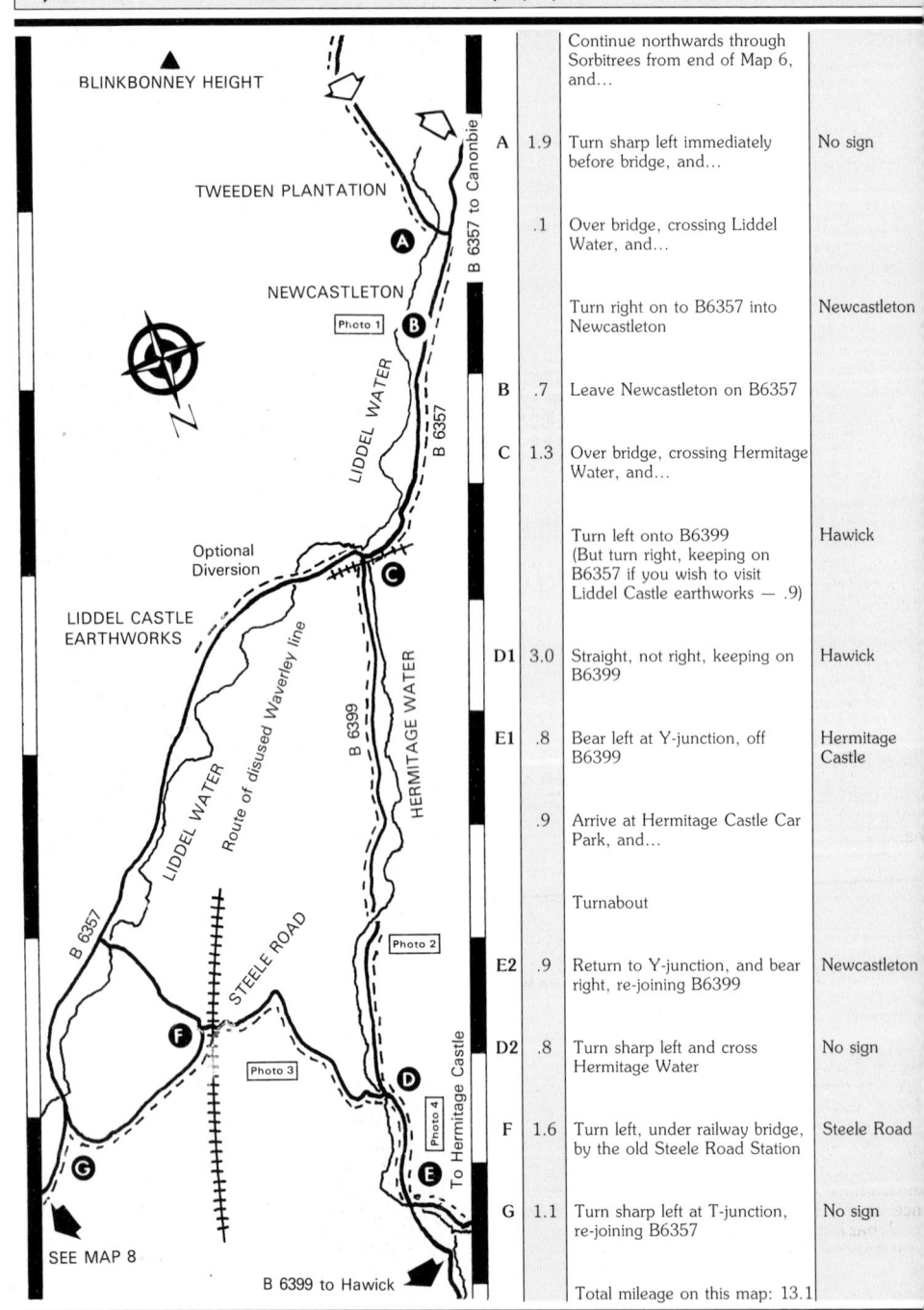

Map 7

	Ref	Miles	Directions	Sign-posted
			Continue northwards through Sorbitrees from end of Map 6, and...	
	A	1.9	Turn sharp left immediately before bridge, and...	No sign
		.1	Over bridge, crossing Liddel Water, and...	
			Turn right on to B6357 into Newcastleton	Newcastleton
	B	.7	Leave Newcastleton on B6357	
	C	1.3	Over bridge, crossing Hermitage Water, and...	
			Turn left onto B6399 (But turn right, keeping on B6357 if you wish to visit Liddel Castle earthworks — .9)	Hawick
	D1	3.0	Straight, not right, keeping on B6399	Hawick
	E1	.8	Bear left at Y-junction, off B6399	Hermitage Castle
		.9	Arrive at Hermitage Castle Car Park, and...	
			Turnabout	
	E2	.9	Return to Y-junction, and bear right, re-joining B6399	Newcastleton
	D2	.8	Turn sharp left and cross Hermitage Water	No sign
	F	1.6	Turn left, under railway bridge, by the old Steele Road Station	Steele Road
	G	1.1	Turn sharp left at T-junction, re-joining B6357	No sign
			Total mileage on this map: 13.1	

On Route

Map 7

Firmly ensconced in 'Steel Bonnet Country' the brooding fells provide a perfect foil to the gentle, tree-covered gorges of Liddelwater. The hardware of this era still remains as a grim reminder of centuries past. Massive brooding fortifications like Hermitage and equally expansive, yet leaving more to the imagination, the grass-covered motte and bailey earthworks of Liddel Castle. A pleasant but intriguing surprise to stumble upon is the regimented "new" village of Newcastleton.

1. Newcastleton

Newcastleton

The village of Newcastleton is of no great age being built in 1793 by the third Duke of Buccleuch to house the border weavers. It was visited by Sir Walter Scott when he was researching for his Border ballads. A major folk festival is held here each July.

Liddel Castle (Optional diversion)

Only massive earthworks remain by the side of the B6357 road but they are impressive none the less, towering high above the vertical tree clad gorge of Liddelwater. The proximity of the Roman road leads historians to believe the site was occupied during the Roman occupation. The size of the earthwork is surprising covering almost four acres with ditches some six feet wide. In the field on the opposite side of the road is the base of an ancient cross.

2. The original landscape of the Borders

Hermitage Castle

Although roofless the interior is in good repair. The castle dates from the 13th century, although the 15th century Douglas Clan were responsible for the massive exterior walls. Romance surrounds the site's occupation by Lord William Soulis reputed an evil wizard who was boiled to death in a cauldron. Two miles north east of the castle is a circle of stones at Nine Stone Rig reputed to be the scene of his cannibalistic fate. Royal visitors to Hermitage include Mary Queen of Scots in 1566, and Sir Walter Scott who firmly declared the fortification his "favourite castle".

3. The new landscape of the Borders

Steele Road and the Waverley Line

A railway bridge over the road marks the route, not of a country branchline, but what was one of the three main routes between London and Edinburgh. It is hard now to credit that main line expresses and sleepers brought their passengers into this wild landscape, but so it was. Now the area which was once served by the station in the hamlet of Steele Road, has returned to almost the state of isolation that existed before the coming of the railway. Here too, the forests are being extended over the hills that once reared sheep.

4. Hermitage Castle

15

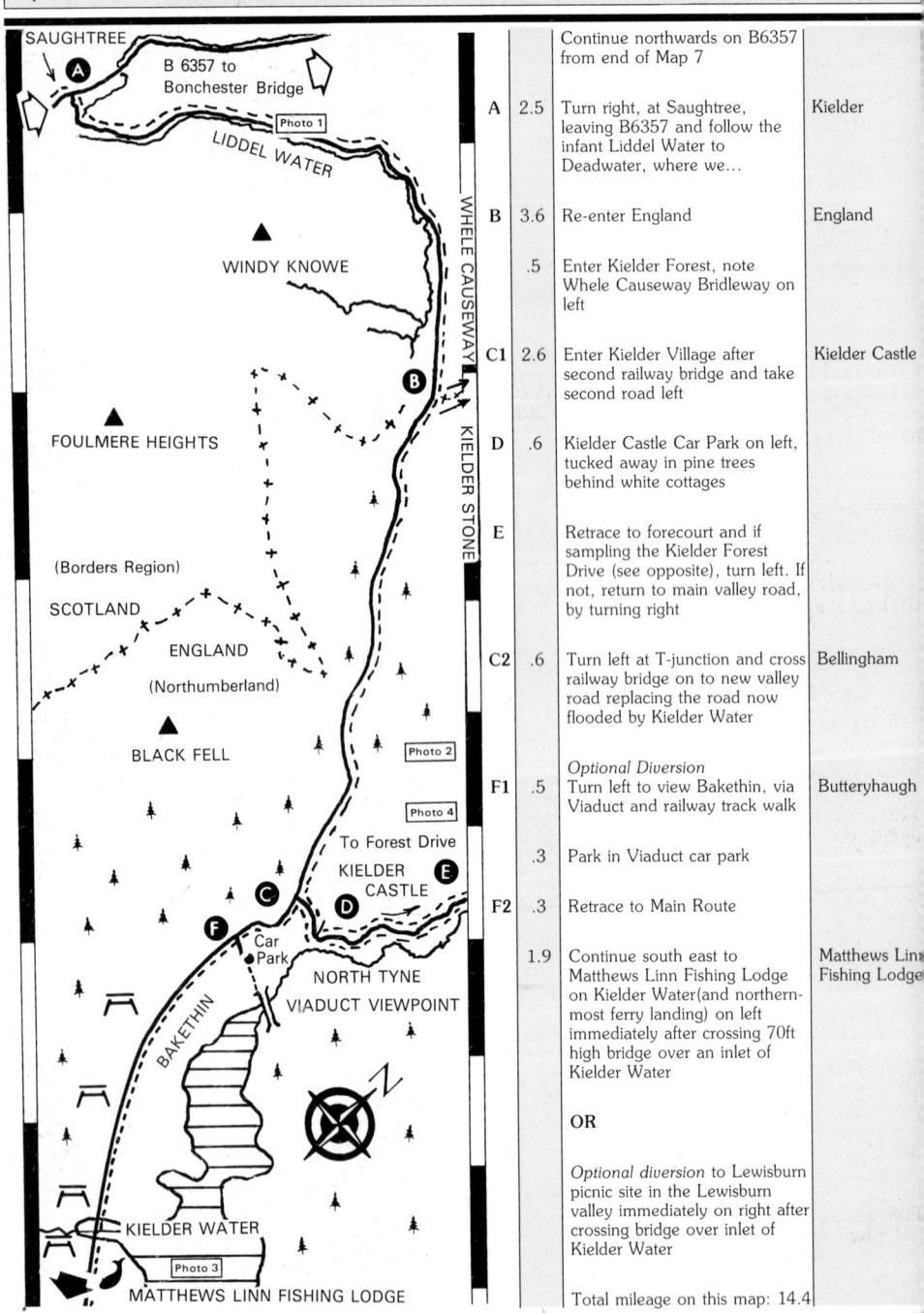

Map 8

	Miles	kms Ref. Miles	Directions	Sign-posted
			Continue northwards on B6357 from end of Map 7	
	A	2.5	Turn right, at Saughtree, leaving B6357 and follow the infant Liddel Water to Deadwater, where we...	Kielder
	B	3.6	Re-enter England	England
		.5	Enter Kielder Forest, note Whele Causeway Bridleway on left	
	C1	2.6	Enter Kielder Village after second railway bridge and take second road left	Kielder Castle
	D	.6	Kielder Castle Car Park on left, tucked away in pine trees behind white cottages	
	E		Retrace to forecourt and if sampling the Kielder Forest Drive (see opposite), turn left. If not, return to main valley road, by turning right	
	C2	.6	Turn left at T-junction and cross railway bridge on to new valley road replacing the road now flooded by Kielder Water	Bellingham
			Optional Diversion	
	F1	.5	Turn left to view Bakethin, via Viaduct and railway track walk	Butteryhaugh
		.3	Park in Viaduct car park	
	F2	.3	Retrace to Main Route	
		1.9	Continue south east to Matthews Linn Fishing Lodge on Kielder Water (and northern-most ferry landing) on left immediately after crossing 70ft high bridge over an inlet of Kielder Water	Matthews Linn Fishing Lodge
			OR	
			Optional diversion to Lewisburn picnic site in the Lewisburn valley immediately on right after crossing bridge over inlet of Kielder Water	
			Total mileage on this map: 14.4	

CROWN COPYRIGHT RESERVED

On Route

Map 8

The route follows the infant Liddel Water to its source in the appropriately named low summit of Deadwater, on the border between Scotland and England. Immediately on crossing the border the most stately trees of Kielder Forest are reached. Here it was in 1926 that the Forestry Commission planted an open moorland, the first trees of which now form Kielder and the Border forests — which today form the largest man-made forest in Europe. Since 1974 a second massive transformation has taken place in the North Tyne Valley — the construction of a dam which has resulted in Kielder Water — an area of water larger than Ullswater.

Kielder Village

After a scattering of houses built in the 1920s, a new village was planned in the 1930s but commencement was only possible after World War II. It was hoped that it would eventually have a population of over 1,000, but mechanisation of forestry in the intervening years has lead to drastic reductions in labour requirements, and the village could not grow as planned. However the development of Kielder Water and all its recreation facilities will bring new life to the village and area.

Kielder Castle

This was originally a shooting lodge of the Duke of Northumberland — who sold the North Tyne Valley farms to the Forestry Commission in the 1920s. Today the Castle houses a Forest Museum and Information Centre and there is a Craft Shop and Cafe — all open in the tourist season.

Kielder-Byrness Forest Drive

From the forecourt of the Castle is an unsurfaced 11 mile forest road through the forest and over high moors to link on to the A68 in Redesdale (see Key Map). A modest toll is charged and the road is closed from the end of October until Easter, at times of high fire hazard and when weather makes the surface unsuitable.

Bakethin Reservoir

Half a mile S.E. of Kielder Village is the northern end of Bakethin, a reservoir upstream of the main Kielder Water. The southern shore, and southern half of Bakethin is a nature reserve from which the public is excluded. Fishing is allowed in the northern half and there is an excellent walk along the old North Tyne Railway from the Viaduct and Fishing Lodge Car Park.

Matthews Linn and Lewis Burn

Our road crosses an inlet of the lake on a 70' high bridge. To the north is Matthews Linn — the major Fishing Lodge near the head of Kielder Water and the outer terminus of the ferry.

To the south a forest road leads up the enchanting Lewis Burn to a picnic site and forest walks provided by the Forestry Commission.

1. Liddel Water

2. Kielder Castle

3. Gowanburn and Wilderness North Shore

4. Kielder Forest

17

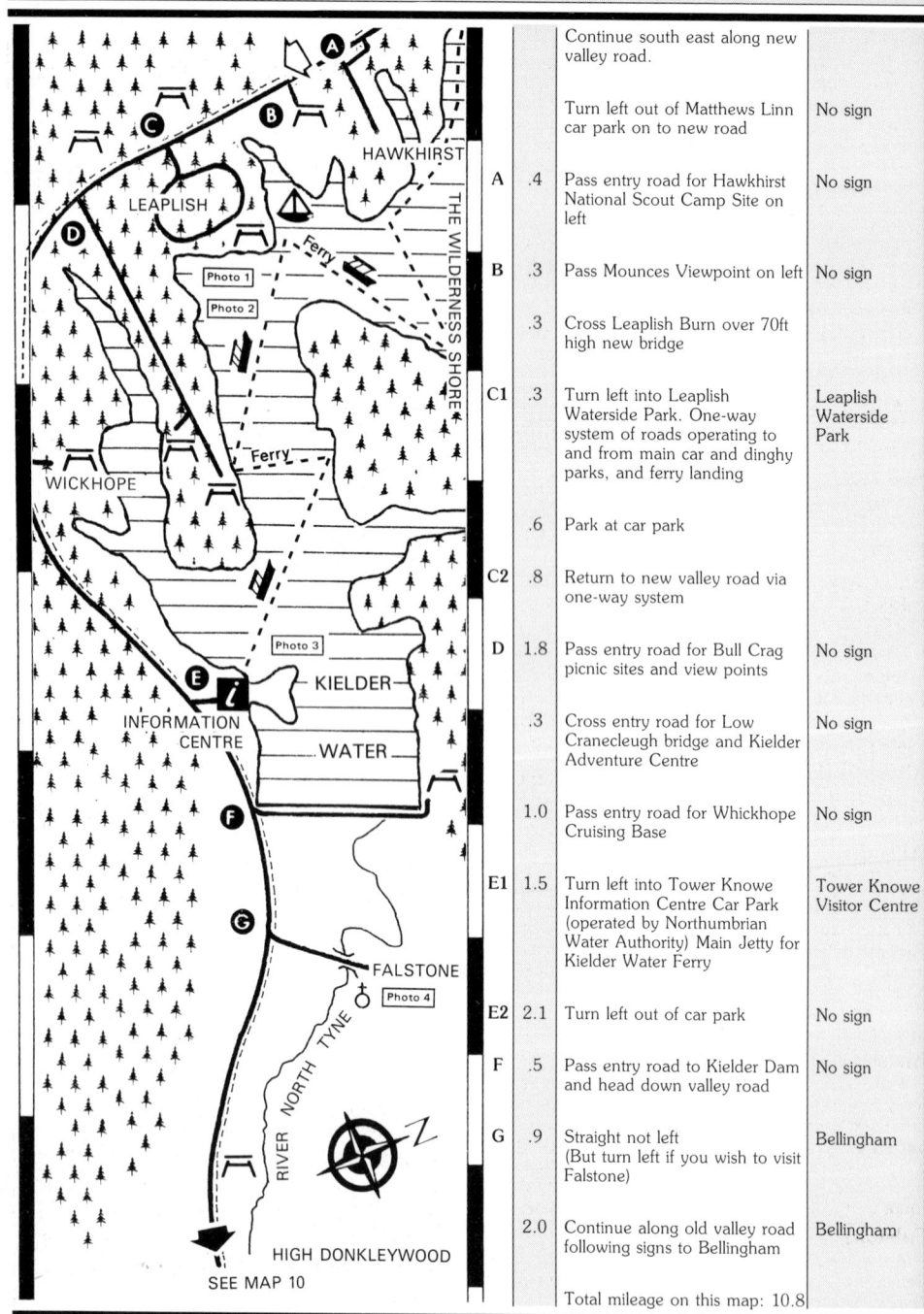

Map 9

Ref	kms Miles	Directions	Sign-posted
		Continue south east along new valley road.	
		Turn left out of Matthews Linn car park on to new road	No sign
A	.4	Pass entry road for Hawkhirst National Scout Camp Site on left	No sign
B	.3	Pass Mounces Viewpoint on left	No sign
	.3	Cross Leaplish Burn over 70ft high new bridge	
C1	.3	Turn left into Leaplish Waterside Park. One-way system of roads operating to and from main car and dinghy parks, and ferry landing	Leaplish Waterside Park
	.6	Park at car park	
C2	.8	Return to new valley road via one-way system	
D	1.8	Pass entry road for Bull Crag picnic sites and view points	No sign
	.3	Cross entry road for Low Cranecleugh bridge and Kielder Adventure Centre	No sign
	1.0	Pass entry road for Whickhope Cruising Base	No sign
E1	1.5	Turn left into Tower Knowe Information Centre Car Park (operated by Northumbrian Water Authority) Main Jetty for Kielder Water Ferry	Tower Knowe Visitor Centre
E2	2.1	Turn left out of car park	No sign
F	.5	Pass entry road to Kielder Dam and head down valley road	No sign
G	.9	Straight not left (But turn left if you wish to visit Falstone)	Bellingham
	2.0	Continue along old valley road following signs to Bellingham	Bellingham
		Total mileage on this map: 10.8	

CROWN COPYRIGHT RESERVED

On Route

Map 9

From Matthews Linn Fishing Lodge a valley road sweeps in and out of the tall pine trees giving extensive views of Kielder Water. Never near the shore of Kielder Water, the numerous side roads to the various attractions and facilities entice the visitor. East of the dam, the route follows the former valley road in the lush valley bottom.

Hawkhirst Peninsula

This totally wooded headland has been developed by the Scouts Association as their second largest outdoor pursuits centre in Britain.

Mounces Viewpoint

This is a skilfully constructed viewpoint on an open hill top from which the longest reach of Kielder Water can be viewed to the east.

Leaplish

This is probably the busiest part of the new Kielder Water. The ferry calls here on request, and boat and dinghy hire is centred here. Kielder Water Sailing Club is also based here and visitors can become temporary members to enjoy the facilities. The "Beeches" route is a most attractive walk from the Leaplish Car Park, giving marvellous views.

Bull Crag

Bull Crag is a two mile peninsula between the main Kielder Water and the Whickhope Inlet. Picnic sites, parking places, walks and viewpoints abound.

Tower Knowe Information Centre and Ferry Landing

On a magnificent heather moorland the Water Authority has provided an Information Centre, cafe and plenty of car and coach parking.

A short walk to the viewpoint on Tower Knowe Headland impresses the scale of Kielder Water on the visitor. The wilderness north shore can be seen from here, and as this area has no roads, pony trekking and walking should only be undertaken by those with experience. The ferry service is based at Tower Knowe Landing and it is from here that most visitors embark — for a round trip, or for a short trip to one of the other four intermediate landings, including two on the north shore. It is from one of the ferries that Kielder Water can most easily be viewed. To walk the shortline is almost thirty miles taking into account the distance round the deep inlets.

Kielder Dam

The water behind Kielder Dam is as deep as the height of Nelson's Column. It is usually possible to drive across the dam to the north abutment car park but access to the shore at this point is not allowed. A way-marked walk to Kielder Village on the wild north side of the reservoir is proposed, but much of the route is tough-going and really only for the hardy.

Falstone

A secluded village of great antiquity its name being derived from the Anglo Saxon word for stronghold "Fausten".

1. Shore Fishing — Keilder Water

2. Leaplish Waterside Park

3. Ferry on Kielder Water

4. Falstone Church

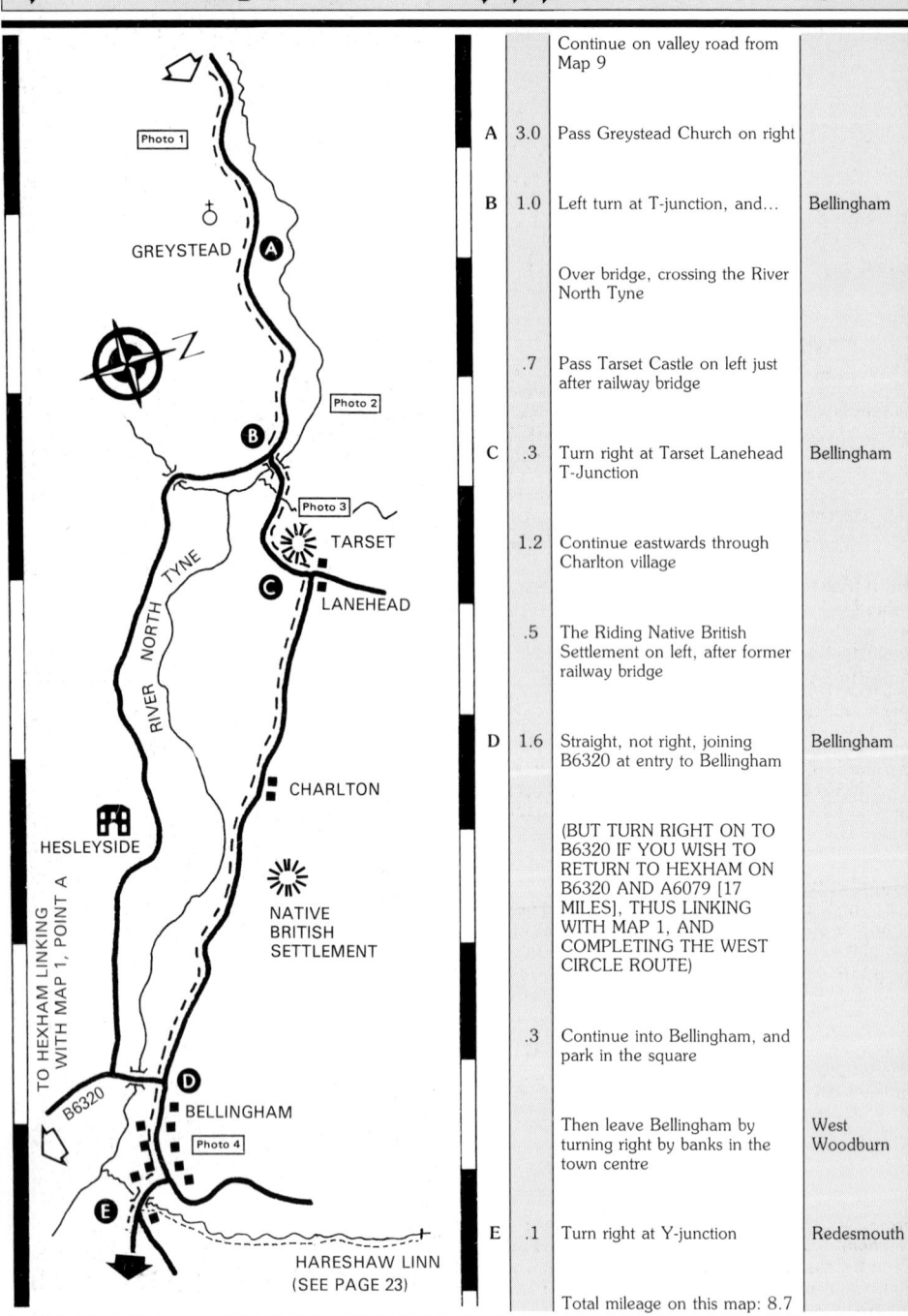

Map 10

Miles	kms Ref. Miles	Directions	Sign-posted

		Continue on valley road from Map 9	
A	3.0	Pass Greystead Church on right	
B	1.0	Left turn at T-junction, and...	Bellingham
		Over bridge, crossing the River North Tyne	
	.7	Pass Tarset Castle on left just after railway bridge	
C	.3	Turn right at Tarset Lanehead T-Junction	Bellingham
	1.2	Continue eastwards through Charlton village	
	.5	The Riding Native British Settlement on left, after former railway bridge	
D	1.6	Straight, not right, joining B6320 at entry to Bellingham	Bellingham
		(BUT TURN RIGHT ON TO B6320 IF YOU WISH TO RETURN TO HEXHAM ON B6320 AND A6079 [17 MILES], THUS LINKING WITH MAP 1, AND COMPLETING THE WEST CIRCLE ROUTE)	
	.3	Continue into Bellingham, and park in the square	
		Then leave Bellingham by turning right by banks in the town centre	West Woodburn
E	.1	Turn right at Y-junction	Redesmouth
		Total mileage on this map: 8.7	

Map labels: Photo 1, GREYSTEAD, A, Photo 2, B, Photo 3, TARSET, C, LANEHEAD, RIVER NORTH TYNE, HESLEYSIDE, CHARLTON, NATIVE BRITISH SETTLEMENT, D, BELLINGHAM, Photo 4, B6320, TO HEXHAM LINKING WITH MAP 1, POINT A, E, HARESHAW LINN (SEE PAGE 23)

CROWN COPYRIGHT RESERVED

On Route

Map 10

Leaving the Border Forests behind, the route continues down the North Tyne Valley, accompanying the infant river, increasing with every tributary. The moors are never far away — and this is now great holiday pony trekking country — formerly the haunts of moss troopers and reivers raiding in earnest. Here are the grass covered mounds which overlay the remains of Tarset Castle dating from 1267, while on the opposite side of the river can be glimpsed Hesleyside — a classical country house of the 17th century.

Tarset Castle

The castle of which only a few stones and grass covered mounds remain, was first constructed in 1267 by the Black Comyn, Lord of Badenock. He was the father of the even more notorious Red Comyn who was a contender for the throne of Scotland until he met a bloody end at Dumfries during a difference of opinion with Robert Bruce in 1306. Tarset Castle was finally destroyed by reivers from Liddesdale who fired it in the 16th century.

The Riding — A Native British Settlement

Shortly after Charlton Village on the north side of the road and across the track bed of the old Border Counties Railway, which linked Hexham and Riccarton Junction on the Waverley line, is the remains of an old Native British Settlement. The area of western Northumberland contains a number of such settlements, predating the occupation by the Romans — but no site is yet displayed or interpreted. However, the setting now grown around with hardwood trees — not planted imported conifers — is quite pleasant, and an appreciation of the fortified position can be obtained by those with imagination.

Bellingham (See also page 23)

The small, largely stone built, town of Bellingham of under 1,000 people, serves as the market centre for a vast area of west Northumberland's forest and farming villages in North Tynedale and Redesdale.

Its importance to the area belies its size. In spite of the largest man-made forest in Europe being on its doorstep, Bellingham is still noted for its autumn sales of sheep and cattle bred on the surrounding hills.

These hills are great walking country, and the Pennine Way passes through the town — 30 miles to Kirk Yetholm in Scotland, and 220 miles to the southern end, at Edale in Derbyshire.

From Bellingham it is possible to return direct to Hexham — only 17 miles down the leafy North Tyne Valley, via B6320. But for more information about Bellingham and to continue the longer tour via Wallington Hall and Corbridge, see page 23.

1. North Tyne Valley

2. North Tyne Valley, Tarset

3. Bridge over the Tarset Burn near Lanehead

4. Bellingham Mart

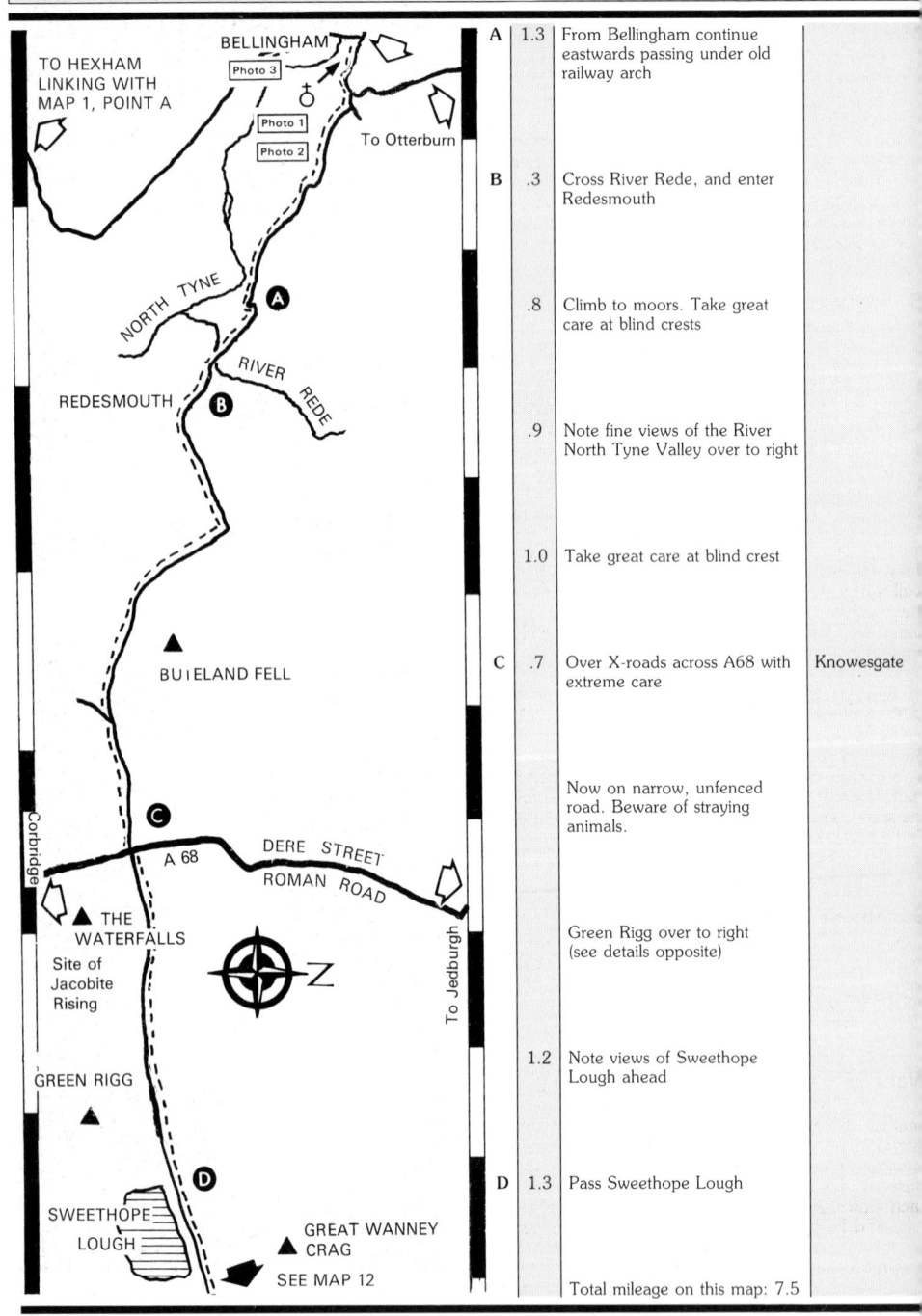

Map 11

Miles / kms Ref. Miles / Directions / Signposted

Map labels:
- BELLINGHAM
- TO HEXHAM LINKING WITH MAP 1, POINT A
- Photo 3
- Photo 1
- Photo 2
- To Otterburn
- NORTH TYNE
- RIVER REDE
- REDESMOUTH
- BUTELAND FELL
- Corbridge
- A 68
- DERE STREET ROMAN ROAD
- To Jedburgh
- THE WATERFALLS
- Site of Jacobite Rising
- GREEN RIGG
- SWEETHOPE LOUGH
- GREAT WANNEY CRAG
- SEE MAP 12

Ref	Miles	Directions	Sign-posted
A	1.3	From Bellingham continue eastwards passing under old railway arch	
B	.3	Cross River Rede, and enter Redesmouth	
	.8	Climb to moors. Take great care at blind crests	
	.9	Note fine views of the River North Tyne Valley over to right	
	1.0	Take great care at blind crest	
C	.7	Over X-roads across A68 with extreme care	Knowesgate
		Now on narrow, unfenced road. Beware of straying animals.	
		Green Rigg over to right (see details opposite)	
	1.2	Note views of Sweethope Lough ahead	
D	1.3	Pass Sweethope Lough	
		Total mileage on this map: 7.5	

CROWN COPYRIGHT RESERVED

On Route

Map 11

After Bellingham the route from Redesmouth climbs over the rolling countryside of Buteland Fell, following the line of the former railway. Across the A68 running north along the route of Roman Dere Street, the route continues over high ground at Green Rigg. Then the infant River Wansbeck descends into the shimmering rush-lined waters of Sweethope Lough. (It is possible to join the route at Bellingham direct from Chesters — see Map 1, Point E, on page 2.)

1. Long Pack Grave, Bellingham

Bellingham (See also page 21)

The church of St. Cuthbert dates from the beginning of the 13th century and incorporates a unique stone roof, a measure against the conflagrations of the Scots who twice succeeded in razing the church to the ground. In the churchyard behind the Black Bull is the Long Pack Grave and down a narrow lane by the side of the church is St. Cuthbert's Well, known locally as Cuddy's Well, and which is featured in local legends. In complete contrast is the 2-mile nature trail up Hareshaw Linn which culminates in one of Northumbria's most spectacular waterfalls cascading some 30 feet into a deep chasm. The route is quite tortuous in places but well signposted. Make sure you go all the way along the route and do not be misled into thinking smaller waterfalls on the way are the real thing. (See Map 10, page 20.)

2. Stone Roof, Bellingham Church

Green Rigg

On this desolate high ground overlooking Sweethope Lough, the country's Jacobite supporters planned to enter combat against the House of Hanover on October 6th 1715. The hill, half a mile to the south, known as Waterfalls is the point where the Earl of Derwentwater held council. Nearby is the source of the River Wansbeck.

Sweethope Lough

Although the lake is private, rambles on the moorland around its perimeter include a delightful walk to Redesdale, and fishing permits can be obtained from nearby Lake House or the Percy Arms Hotel, Otterburn.

Wanney Crags or Wild Hills O'Wanney

To the north of Sweethope Lough, the soft heather-clad upland, broken by a pine plantation is overlooked by the "Wild Hills O'Wanny's", a great outcrop of sandstone with a vertical descent to the west. Romantic names have been bestowed upon each outcrop — Great Wanny, Little Wanay, Aird Law and Hepple Heugh. The more energetic visitor who treks across the moors to these peaks will be rewarded with views of the surrounding hills as far as the Cheviot Hills marking the border with Scotland.

3. Hareshaw Linn, Bellingham

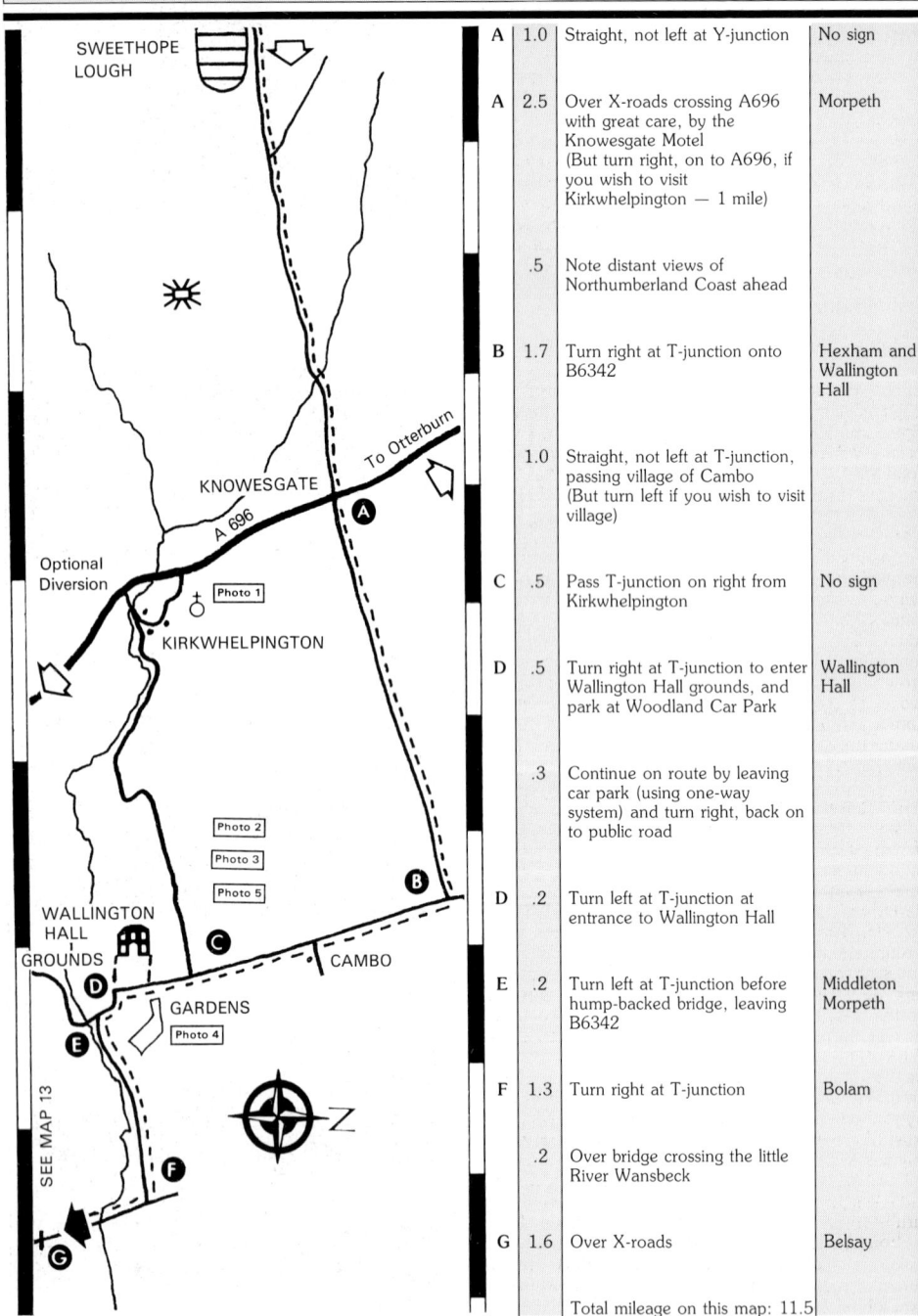

Map 12

	k·ms Ref Miles	Directions	Sign-posted
A	1.0	Straight, not left at Y-junction	No sign
A	2.5	Over X-roads crossing A696 with great care, by the Knowesgate Motel (But turn right, on to A696, if you wish to visit Kirkwhelpington — 1 mile)	Morpeth
	.5	Note distant views of Northumberland Coast ahead	
B	1.7	Turn right at T-junction onto B6342	Hexham and Wallington Hall
	1.0	Straight, not left at T-junction, passing village of Cambo (But turn left if you wish to visit village)	
C	.5	Pass T-junction on right from Kirkwhelpington	No sign
D	.5	Turn right at T-junction to enter Wallington Hall grounds, and park at Woodland Car Park	Wallington Hall
	.3	Continue on route by leaving car park (using one-way system) and turn right, back on to public road	
D	.2	Turn left at T-junction at entrance to Wallington Hall	
E	.2	Turn left at T-junction before hump-backed bridge, leaving B6342	Middleton Morpeth
F	1.3	Turn right at T-junction	Bolam
	.2	Over bridge crossing the little River Wansbeck	
G	1.6	Over X-roads	Belsay

Total mileage on this map: 11.5

CROWN COPYRIGHT RESERVED

On Route

Map 12

The scenery on the first part of the route is varied and dramatic. To the north and west the stark rolling moors, to the south and east the softer pastureland of large estates and historic demesnes of which Wallington is one of the finest in the North of England. This is the area into which Lancelot 'Capability' Brown was born, and in which he grew to manhood. He gained experience on the landscape of Kirkharle, near Wallington, before moving southwards to Stowe in Buckinghamshire, where he was soon working under the great William Kent — at the start of his own illustrious career.

Kirkwhelpington (Optional diversion)

St. Bartholemew's church, on its mound above the rest of the village, dates from the 13th century. Now long and narrow, it is much smaller than it once was, with aisles and transepts having been demolished many years ago. Sir Charles Parsons, inventor of the steam turbine, was buried in the churchyard in 1931, and there is a wall monument to him in the church.

Cambo

Attractively situated village lying just ot the north of the Wallington estate, this is largely the creation of the owners of Wallington. There are terraces of estate cottages, but the nearby Tower House is medieval in origin. The church is mid-19th century, with a handsome west tower added in 1883. Capability Brown, who was born in 1716 at Kirkharle, a hamlet two miles to the south-west, went to school at Cambo. In the course of his distinguished career he designed over 120 parks and in 1765 he carried out some work at Wallington Hall.

Wallington Hall

This is the largest National Trust Estate in the North of England and certainly Northumberland's piece de resistance. Built in 1688 the Hall has interiors dating from the mid 18th century. Superb rococo plasterwork sets off fine porcelain and needlework exhibits. The Central Hall was added in the 19th century and the world famous wall paintings depicting Northumbrian scenes by William Bell Scott and other decor by Ruskin attract visitors from all over the world. Scott's paintings vividly depict milestones in the history of Northumbria. Wallington was the home of the Trevelyan family since 1777 and was given to the National Trust by Sir Charles Trevelyan in 1942. An added attraction is a display of doll's houses and toy soldiers. The Clock Tower incorporates a National Trust Shop and restaurant. There is also a display of coaches in the West Coach Houses.

The Hall is set in 100 acres of amenity woodlands and lakes, and there is a delightful walled garden with shrubs and a conservatory, all at some distance from the house, and approached down a wooded pathway beside a small stream. The stone griffins' heads, standing in front of the house near the road, were brought here by sea from London in 1760.

1. Kirkwhelpington Church

2. Wallington Hall

3. Clock Tower, Wallington

4. Walled Garden, Wallington

5. Griffins at Wallington

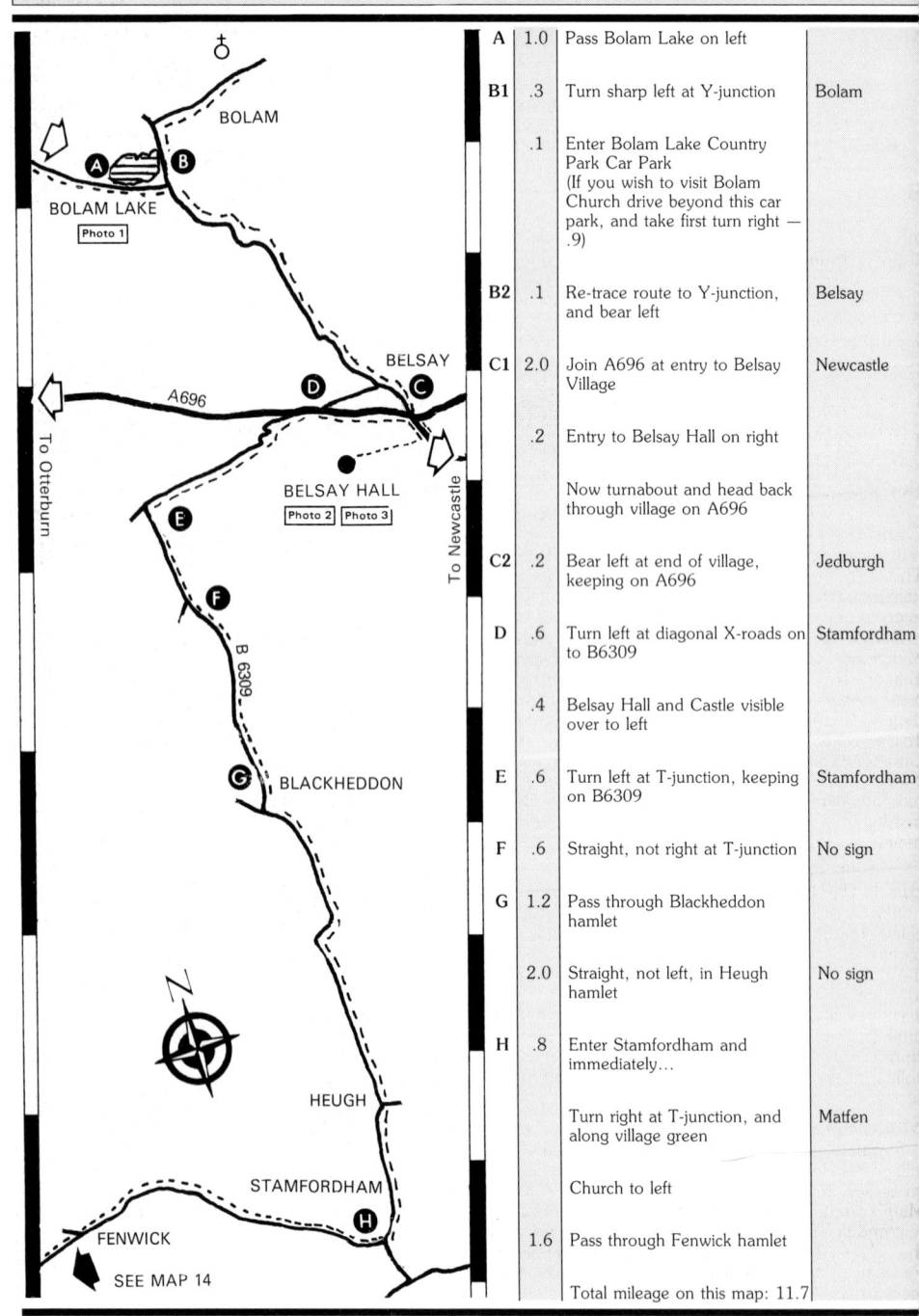

Map 13

Ref	kms/Miles	Directions	Signposted
A	1.0	Pass Bolam Lake on left	
B1	.3	Turn sharp left at Y-junction	Bolam
	.1	Enter Bolam Lake Country Park Car Park (If you wish to visit Bolam Church drive beyond this car park, and take first turn right — .9)	
B2	.1	Re-trace route to Y-junction, and bear left	Belsay
C1	2.0	Join A696 at entry to Belsay Village	Newcastle
	.2	Entry to Belsay Hall on right	
		Now turnabout and head back through village on A696	
C2	.2	Bear left at end of village, keeping on A696	Jedburgh
D	.6	Turn left at diagonal X-roads on to B6309	Stamfordham
	.4	Belsay Hall and Castle visible over to left	
E	.6	Turn left at T-junction, keeping on B6309	Stamfordham
F	.6	Straight, not right at T-junction	No sign
G	1.2	Pass through Blackheddon hamlet	
	2.0	Straight, not left, in Heugh hamlet	No sign
H	.8	Enter Stamfordham and immediately...	
		Turn right at T-junction, and along village green	Matfen
		Church to left	
	1.6	Pass through Fenwick hamlet	
		Total mileage on this map: 11.7	

CROWN COPYRIGHT RESERVED

On Route

Map 13

A journey through meandering byways calling at several interesting churches, notably at Bolam and Stamfordham, and also an opportunity for a picnic by Bolam Lake. However the outstanding place of interest on this route is Belsay Hall, and this should certainly not be missed.

Bolam Lake Country Park

The bol or hill town was once a bustling place inhabited by more than 200 families. Now only the church, Bolam Hall, a private residence and the picturesque artificial lake remain. The Hall stands on the site of a medieval castle and the church of St. Andrew dates from Saxon times. On the moor to the west of the church is a mysteriously grooved standing stone, known as Poind and his Man. Less than a mile from the church towards Belsay lies Bolam Lake, a shimmering stretch of man-made water designed by the famous Newcastle architect, John Dobson in 1818. Visitors are welcome to picnic by the water's edge and fishing is available.

Belsay and Belsay Hall

The old village of Belsay was situated between the Castle and the new Hall, and was demolished and replaced by the new village in the 1830s and 1840s. This is distinguished by ground-floor arcading in the Italian manner, and at least makes a change from every other village on our journey.

Belsay has been continuously occupied by the Middletons, the family whose forbears built the castle in about 1370. This is now a ruin, to which is attached a still habitable Jacobean manor house, and together they make a very impressive sight. However between 1810 and 1817 the family built a fine Hall in the Greek Doric style, to the designs of the young Newcastle architect, John Dobson. The interior of the Hall is beautifully austere and this together with the nearby castle ruins and the picturesque gardens, make a visit here well worthwhile. Shop. Refreshments.

Black Heddon

Villagers will delight in telling of the adventures of a celebrated poltergeist by the name of Silky who regularly appeared in the neighbourhood, notably in the 19th century, on a bridge to the south on the road to Stamfordham. The ghostly figure draped in silks was a wealthy villager who died so suddenly she was unable to disclose the whereabouts of a treasure. One stormy night a ceiling in a house in the village collapsed revealing a calf skin bag of gold and Silky's secret was no more.

Stamfordham and Fenwick

Stamfordham is a stone built village surrounding a village green in the centre of which is a square market cross with four open arches dating from 1736. St. Mary's Church dates from the 13th century, but was restored in 1848. A mile and a quarter after reaching the village the road passes through the hamlet of Fenwick where the remains of an ancient tower are incorporated into a farm.

1. Bolam Lake

2. Belsay Hall   An English Heritage Photograph

3. The Pillar Hall, Belsay Hall
An English Heritage Photograph

Miles	Map 14	kms Ref Miles	Directions	Sign-posted
		1.6	Matfen Hall visible ahead	
	A	.4	Enter Matfen	
			Pass through village, and...	
	B	.2	At far end, bear left	Newcastle
	C	.9	Over offset X-roads (Standing Stone down to left by farm)	No sign
	D	1.3	Turn left at T-junction on to B6318, which follows the line of Hadrian's Wall	Newcastle
	E	.3	Turn right at Y-junction on to B6321	Corbridge
		.7	Shildon Hill over to left	
	F	.2	Over X-roads, keeping on B6321	Corbridge
			Total mileage on this map: 5.6	

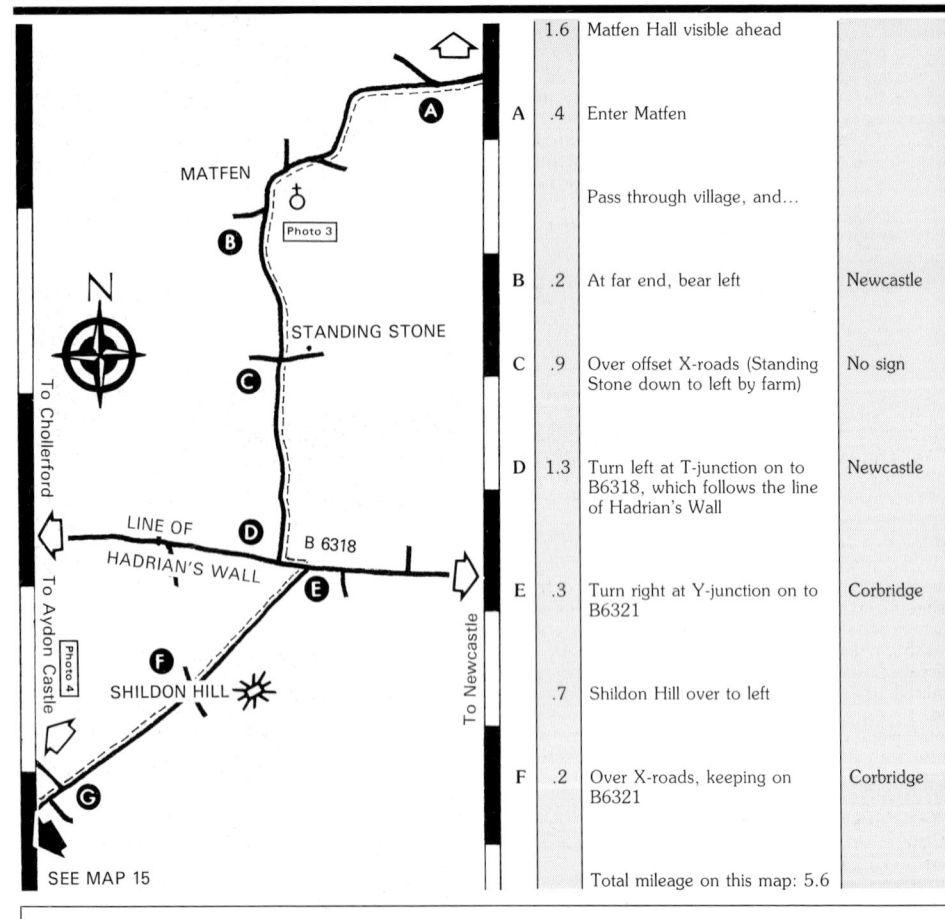

SEE MAP 15

Bath House, Chesters Roman Fort, (See Page 3)

Belsay Hall (See page 27)   An English Heritage Photograph

CROWN COPYRIGHT RESERVED

On Route

Map 14

The tranquillity which pervades this section of route makes it difficult to believe that the bustling city of Newcastle is just fifteen or so miles to the east. Lush greenery abounds in the spacious, typically stone-built village of Matfen with its green. Then a farming landscape of substantial farms and fields formed by the Enclosure Movement is traversed — and Hadrian's Wall, or rather its course, is met again for a short while.

Matfen

The village and its green is dominated by the huge spire of the parish church, built in 1842, the total cost being borne by the philanthropic Northumbrian, Sir Edward Blackett. Matfen Hall is almost totally obscured in a densely wooded park. This superb Gothic masterpiece is now the Northumberland Cheshire Home.

There is a 7-foot-high standing stone at Standing Stone Farm (see route directions, Point C) complete with cup-marks and rings — sure signs of its Bronze Age origins. It is known locally as the Stob Stone.

Hadrian's Wall

An entirely different aspect of Hadrian's Wall is now seen at Matfen road end, where our route turns eastwards for half a mile towards Newcastle. The road is actually built on top of the course of Hadrian's Wall — with the deep ditch immediately to the north, and several defensive parallel shallower ditches and mounds forming the vallum being clearly visible in the fields to the south. Hereabouts the landscape is one dating from the enclosures of the 17th and 18th centuries, with long straight roads and large square fields.

Aydon Castle (see page 30)

Claimed to be one of the finest fortified manor houses in England, Aydon Castle is situated in wild country overlooking the steep wooded valley of the Cor Burn. Dating from the latter half of the 13th century, it is rather an architectural oddity for Northumberland, being built in the style of a medieval manor house more common in the less warlike south of England, by emigré Lincolnshire nobleman, Robert de Reymes. However the original design proved unsuitable in the face of possible attack by the Scots, and fortifications including a substantial outer wall were soon added, following the granting of a licence to crenellate dated 1305.

It was converted into a farmhouse in the 17th century and lived in until as recently as 1966, and it is for these reasons that so much of it has survived. The Great Hall, situated on the first floor and reached by an external staircase, is Aydon's outstanding feature and incorporates many interesting medieval details. Other items worthy of note are the latrine tower, the sheltered orchard overlooking the Cor Burn, and the splendid medieval chimney on the outer wall.

Shop. Refreshments. 'Living History' Education Centre.

1. Market Cross, Stamfordham (see page 27)

2. Stamfordham Church (see page 27)

3. The Village Green, Matfen

4. Aydon Castle   An English Heritage Photograph

29

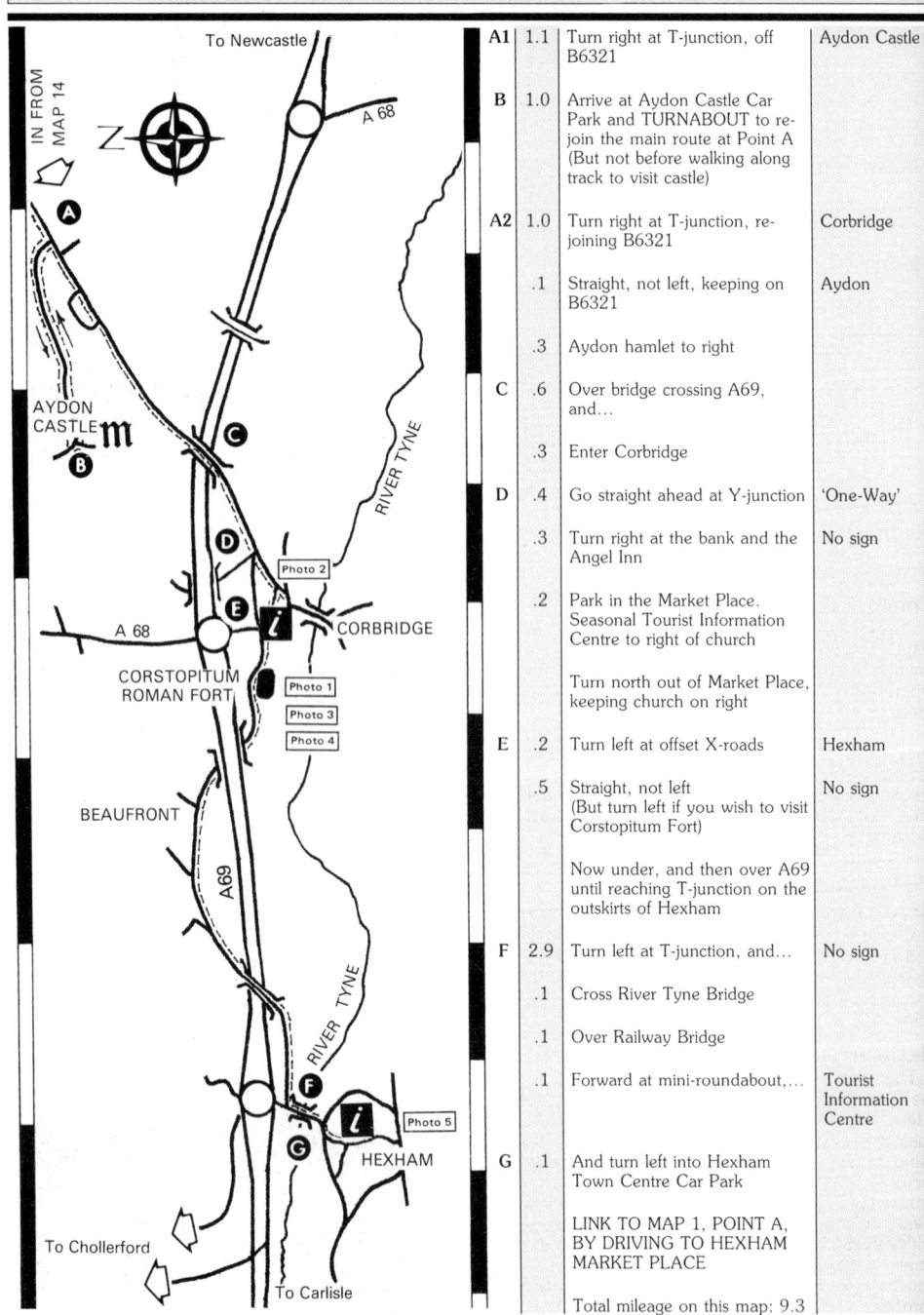

Miles	Map 15	kms Ref Miles	Directions	Sign-posted
		A1 1.1	Turn right at T-junction, off B6321	Aydon Castle
		B 1.0	Arrive at Aydon Castle Car Park and TURNABOUT to re-join the main route at Point A (But not before walking along track to visit castle)	
		A2 1.0	Turn right at T-junction, re-joining B6321	Corbridge
		.1	Straight, not left, keeping on B6321	Aydon
		.3	Aydon hamlet to right	
		C .6	Over bridge crossing A69, and…	
		.3	Enter Corbridge	
		D .4	Go straight ahead at Y-junction	'One-Way'
		.3	Turn right at the bank and the Angel Inn	No sign
		.2	Park in the Market Place. Seasonal Tourist Information Centre to right of church	
			Turn north out of Market Place, keeping church on right	
		E .2	Turn left at offset X-roads	Hexham
		.5	Straight, not left (But turn left if you wish to visit Corstopitum Fort)	No sign
			Now under, and then over A69 until reaching T-junction on the outskirts of Hexham	
		F 2.9	Turn left at T-junction, and…	No sign
		.1	Cross River Tyne Bridge	
		.1	Over Railway Bridge	
		.1	Forward at mini-roundabout,…	Tourist Information Centre
		G .1	And turn left into Hexham Town Centre Car Park	
			LINK TO MAP 1, POINT A, BY DRIVING TO HEXHAM MARKET PLACE	
			Total mileage on this map: 9.3	

CROWN COPYRIGHT RESERVED

On Route

Map 15

Between the small town of Corbridge and its larger neighbour, the market town of Hexham, the route follows the Tyne Valley as it opens out to provide extensive views to the well wooded hillsides across the lush and fertile haughlands. Several large country seats and other more modest houses stand picturesquely on either side of the valley. Just beyond Corbridge, we visit Corstopitum, the fort for the main supply base for Hadrian's Wall, with its interesting remains and fine museum.

1. Corbridge Lion, Corstopitum

Aydon Castle (See page 29)

Corbridge

One of Northumbria's quaintest and most interesting market towns which in the 8th century is believed to have superseded Bamburgh as the capital of this ancient northern Kingdom.

The parish church dates from the 8th century and the Vicar's Pele Tower in the corner of the churchyard is a fine example of a fortified family tower, which today serves as a Tourist Information Centre. The River Tyne flows by the town under a 17th century stone bridge, one of several bridges which have served the town through the centuries.

Corstopitum

Just half a mile west of the centre of Corbridge stand the impressive remains of the Roman fort and town of Corstopitum built at a vital road junction where Dere Street, the 20th century A68, crosses the Stanegate, the Roman road from Newcastle to Carlisle. Both of these roads and the first century fort were built by Agricola (AD 78 – 84) and although several forts were subsequently added, the remains visible today are largely of the third century military town. Do not miss a visit to the most interesting museum, the contents of which includes the fine fountainhead, known as the Corbridge Lion (see illustration) and many other finds from Corstopitum.

2. Corstopitum

Beaufront Castle

Visible to the left of our route between Corbridge and Hexham, this fine Gothic building was designed by the noted Newcastle architect, John Dobson (see also Belsay, page 27). It was built between 1837 and 1841.

3. Granary Corstopitum   *4. Pele Tower, Corbridge*

Hexham (See also Page 3)

The route now returns to its starting point, across the Tyne Bridge — dating from 1785 — giving a most interesting panoramic view of the whole town, set against a backcloth of the well wooded and steeply rising valley side. Hexham abbey is inevitably the focus of attention, standing proudly on the promontory on which the town centre is situated. Hexham, when viewed from the vantage point of the bridge over the Tyne, truly epitomises the character of small north country towns. Your circuit, or circuits if you have undertaken the tour in two parts, is now complete.

5. Hexham Abbey

31

INDEX

Entry	Page
Acomb	2
Allen Banks	4, 5
Askerton Castle	10, 11
Askerton Park Medieval Landscape	10, 11
Auchope Cairn	13
Aydon Castle	29, 30
Bakethin Viaduct/Viewpoint	16, 17
Banks East Turret	8, 9
Bardon Mill	4
Bellingham	19, 20, 21, 22, 23
Belsay	26, 27
Belsay Hall and Castle	27
Bewcastle	10, 11, 12, 13
Bewshaugh Viewpoint	16, 17
Birdoswald Fort	8, 9, 11
Blackpool Gate	12, 13
Black Heddon	26, 27
Black Lyne	12, 13
Bolam Lake Country Park	26, 27
Border Forest Museum	16, 17
Brocolitia	4, 5
Brown, Lancelot (Capability)	25
Brunton Turret	2, 3
Bull Crag Picnic Sites	18, 19
Byrness Forest Drive	16, 17
Cambo	25
Camboglanna	8, 9
Capability Brown	25
Carrawburgh	4, 5
Carvoran Museum of the Roman Army	6, 7
Catrail	17
Cawfields	6, 7
Chesters Fort	2, 3
Cheviot	13, 25
Chollerford	2, 3
Cilurnum	2, 3
Clock Tower, Wallington	25
Corbridge	28, 30, 31
Corstopitum	30, 31
Coventina's Well	5
Crag Lough	7
Cuddy's Crag	5
Cuddy's Well	23
Deadwater	17
Dere Street	23
de Reymes, Robert	29
Dobson, John	27, 31
Duke of Buccleugh	15
Duke of Northumberland	17
Enclosure Landscape	29
Falstone	18, 19
Fenwick	26, 27
Forest Drive Kielder	16, 17
Gilsland	8
Great Wanney	23
Greenhead	8
Green Rigg	22, 23
Hadrian's Wall	12, 13
Haltwhistle	6, 7
Hare Hill	8, 9, 10, 11
Hareshaw Linn	23
Hawkhirst National Scout Camp Centre	18, 19
Heavenfield	2
Hermitage Castle	14, 15
Heugh	26
Hexham	2, 3, 30, 31
Housesteads	4, 5
Irthing Bridge (Willowford)	8, 9
Kershope Bridge	12, 13
Kershope Burn	12, 13
Kershope Forest	12, 13
Kielder Castle Information Centre	16, 17
Kielder Forest Drive	16, 17
Kielder Forest Information Centre	16, 17
Kielder Village	16, 17
Kielder Water	16, 17, 18, 19
Kielder Water Ferry	18, 19
Kinmont Willie	13
Kirkharle	25
Kirkwhelpington	24, 25
Knowesgate	24, 25
Lanercost Priory	8, 9
Larriston Fell	13
Leahill Turret	8, 9
Leaplish Waterside Park	18, 19
Lewisburn	16, 17
Liddel Castle	14, 15
Liddel Water	14, 15, 16, 17
Little Wanney	23
Longbyre	8
Long Pack Grave	23
Lord William Soulis	15
Maiden's Way	11
Mary, Queen of Scots	15
Matfen	29, 30
Matthews Linn Fishing Lodge	16, 17
Medieval Landscape Askerton Park	10, 11
Middle March Centre	3
Middleton Family	27
Milecastle Inn	6
Mounces Viewpoint	18, 19
Museum of the Roman Army (Carvoran)	6, 7
Museums on Roman Sites:	
Corstopitum	30, 31
Chesters	2, 3
Housesteads	4, 5
Vindolanda	6, 7
Native British Villages	2, 3, 20, 21
Newcastleton	14, 15
National Park	2
National Park Information Centre	6
Parsons, Sir Charles	25
Plankey Mill	5
Poltross Burn Milecastle	8, 9
Pont River	27
Redesmouth	22, 23
Rede River	23
Ridley Hall	5
Robert Bruce	19
Roman Army Museum	7
Saughtree	16, 17
School Hill, Native British Village	2, 3
Scott, William Bell	25
Sewingshields	4, 5
Shield-on-the-Wall	4
Shopford	10, 11
Silky's Bridge	27
Silky the Poltergeist	27
Sir Walter Scott	15
Sorbitrees	14
Stamfordham	26, 27
Stanegate	4, 7
Steele Road	14, 15
Steel Rigg	6, 7
St. Bartholemew	25
St. Cuthbert	23
St. Cuthbert's Well	23
St. John Lee Church	2, 3
St. Wilfred	3
Stob Stone, The	29
Stowe	25
Sweethope Lough	22, 23
Tarset Burn	20, 21
Tarset Castle	20, 21
Temple of Mithras	5
The Riding Native Settlement	20, 21
Thirlwall Castle	8, 9
Tower Knowe Information Centre	18, 19
Tourist Information Centres:	
Corbridge	30, 31
Hexham	2, 3, 30, 31
Upper Denton	8, 9
Vercovicium (Housesteads)	4, 5
Vindolanda	6, 7
Wall Village	2, 3
Wallington Hall	24, 25
Walltown Crags	6, 7
Wansbeck River	24, 25
Wanney Crags	22, 23
Wheel Causeway	16, 17
Whinn Sill	5, 7
White Lyne Water	13
Willowford	8, 9
Windy Knowe	17